THE
COMING
CONFRONTATION

THE COMING CONFRONTATION

Will the Open Society Survive to 1989?

W. H. CHALONER

NORMAN GASH

F. A. HAYEK

JULIUS GOULD

IVOR PEARCE

MAX HARTWELL

RAYMOND FLETCHER

JO GRIMOND

NIGEL LAWSON

THE DUKE OF EDINBURGH

RALPH HARRIS

ARTHUR SELDON

Published by
THE INSTITUTE OF ECONOMIC AFFAIRS
1978

First published in 1978 by
THE INSTITUTE OF ECONOMIC AFFAIRS
2 Lord North Street, London SW1P 3LB

©The Institute of Economic Affairs 1978

ISBN 0-255 36115-7 (cased edition)
ISBN 0-255 36116-5 (paperback edition)

Printed in England by
Goron Pro-Print Co. Ltd., Lancing, West Sussex
Text set in Monotype Times Roman 11 on 12 pt.

CONTENTS

PREFACE

For 21 years the Institute has, by research and dissemination, kept open discussion of the economic aspects of government and the market thought to have been long settled. Its near 250 studies by approaching 300 authors, mostly from British universities, though increasingly from overseas where British economists had migrated, have analysed a vast range of subjects from recurring inflation and unemployment, through perennial fuel (including nuclear power) and transport, education and medical care, to the minor but indicative fire-fighting and water, blood and animal semen.

NEGLECT OF THE MARKET

The theme has throughout, with variations, been the potential use of an instrument that has been neglected because it evolved organically and spontaneously down the centuries and was not fashioned by man: the market. In 1957 it seemed to us that, especially in the long era of Keynes and his self-asserted followers, the Keynesians, but for around a century since the Fabians in 1884, the market had been relegated to second place behind the state as the generator of production and distributor of its fruits. The Institute therefore set out to re-investigate the market. It sponsored studies to ask two sets of questions: about the

value of the market itself, and about the environment
required to enable it to yield its best results: the law (on
property, units of enterprise, contract, sale of goods,
restraint of trade, etc.) and the institutions (of money,
exchange and trade) created by government.

On the first the studies asked:

is there a market in this commodity (or service)?
if there is, does it work well? if not, why not?
if there is not, why not?
are its defects ("imperfections") inherent and irre-
    mediable?
or are they the outcome of an unsuitable environment?
if so, what less imperfect mechanisms can replace
    the market?
is the state less or more imperfect than the market?

And on the second they asked:

how far is the legal environment appropriate?
if inappropriate, is it the fault of imperfect government?
what can government do to perfect it, or reduce its
    imperfections?
what prevents government from so doing?

Both sets of questions have been refined since 1957.
And the second set is being especially sharpened with
the recent development of the economics of politics,[1]

---

[1] *The Economics of Politics,* Readings 18, IEA, 1978, is based on
an IEA Seminar at which papers were delivered by one of the
Founding Fathers of this new development of economics,
Professor J. M. Buchanan of Virginia, and by five leading
authorities: Professors Albert Breton (Ottawa), Bruno Frey
(Switzerland), A. T. Peacock (Buckingham), C. K. Rowley
(Newcastle) and Jack Wiseman (York); academics in other
faculties also discussed its relevance for their subjects (political
institutions, social administration, etc.).

the machinery through which individuals with sharply varying preferences have to decide the production of common services and jointly used ("public") goods (further discussed in the Prologue).

THE MARKET RETURNS

In 1978 the market is back in full vigour as an analytical device, a criterion by which to judge economic perform-ance, and an alternative to government as generator and distributor of goods and services. Fabian self-confidence has faded. The euphoria of the Beveridge/Bevan/Butler Welfare State has waned. The Keynesians are on the defensive.

Even the remaining critics, sceptics and cynics would reluctantly concede the return of the market into the realm of thought and discussion of ideas, principles, theories and concepts. It is increasingly analysed and taught in universities, polytechnics and schools. It is increasingly familiar in company boardrooms, City parlours, and trade union officials' meetings. It has re-emerged in the press, not least in the mass circula-tion newspapers, and in Parliament. It is no longer ignored among the bureaucrats of Whitehall, not least the Treasury. It is recognised among members of the Cabinet, in which the Prime Minister has rejected Keynesian deficit financing and high taxation to finance the "social wage" and the Chancellor of the Exchequer has confessed to infection by monetarism. It is newly welcomed in the Shadow Cabinet, in which the Leader of the Opposition has made herself the most articulate political expositor and advocate of the market since Churchill, Gladstone, Peel and Pitt, and her chief policy adviser has developed from a late student to an original practitioner with insights that could develop the theory itself. And a former Leader of the Liberal Opposition, and its most considerable figure, speaks in the language of classical English liberalism, assertive, radical and strong against the market-usurping state.[2]

NEW UNDERSTANDING, FAILURE OF ALTERNATIVES, POPULISM

The return of the market derives from four causes. There has been a profound intellectual victory for the idea of the market among the élite in academia,[3] public life, industry and the media. Even capitalists and City men no longer sheer off "market forces" but recognise their relevance, and occasionally have a good word for them. The return of the market has been due indispensably to research and re-education, for there can be no practice without "theory"—reasoning, research, logic, analysis and imaginative judgement in identifying hypotheses likely to yield fruitful conclusions.

Second, it also derives from the failure of the state in managing the economy to avoid inflation and unemployment, its incompetence in supplying goods and services, and its consequent neglect of the functions it must perform, defence and other public goods, and of the only

---

[2] Jo Grimond, *The Common Welfare,* Maurice Temple Smith, 1978.

[3] The latest convert is in the new generation of economists who were not taught market economics but had to discover its power for good by experience in government efforts to control the economy without (or against) it—Alan Budd, *The Politics of Economic Planning,* Fontana/Collins, 1978: "I am aware that in ending by supporting the market I am leaving the company of many of the great and the good."

service it could provide tolerably, the redistribution of purchasing power in cash (or voucher).

Third, the return of the market owes something to the realisation by the new class of state employees, or other recipients of state pay, that the frying pan was less fatal than the fire: suppliers would rather be accountable to customers than to politicians. The doctors and dentists have lessons to teach the teachers, the engineers, the steelmen, the miners and the railwaymen.

Not least, the return of the market is due to the growing recognition of its potentially massive populist appeal, largely neglected by the political scientists who tend to favour the state. The market is more democratic and equitable than the state because differences in income and wealth that decide access to goods and services in the market can be more easily corrected than can differences in cultural, social and political power that decide access in state economy. In the absence of the market the citizen is subjected to intolerable bureaucratic paternalism that is turning to inquisitorial tyranny.

That politicians were late to see this underlying change in attitude from hope in the initially benevolent state (and tolerance of the taxation it consumes) to hostility and resentment is the outcome of their misreading "public opinion" into the writings of opinionated journalists who, in press and broadcasting, confused *public* opinion with their often compassionate but irrelevant *personal* prejudices. "Journalists" may miss the wood of basic public attitudes and aspirations for their stock-in-trade trees of day-to-day "news".

What is more surprising is that egalitarian-inclined scholars and politicians whose sympathies lay with the

common people did not see that in suppressing the
market they were subjecting the people to the vagaries
and mercies of arbitrary power even more difficult to
discipline.[4]

IDEAS, INTERESTS AND PUBLIC POLICY

To intellectual rehabilitation and the failure of state
economy can thus be added the unrealised potential of
the political/populist appeal of the market that politicians in all parties are slowly recognising; though some
may be too late. Yet for social scientists pursuing their
work on these lines there must be two anxieties: with a
common origin.

First, what is the impact of ideas on policy? How long
does it take for ideas to influence men and women with
power to act? And will even good ideas capable of
rendering widespread public good be thwarted by vested
interests that, temporarily at least, stand to lose by their
adoption?

Second, and more immediate, will the pursuit of
thinking that yields argument for the maintenance of
open society be inhibited, discouraged or repressed by
the successive closing of society?

On the first, the thwarting of the market, the latest
development is retrograde. Especially since 1974, but
going further back to the 1960s, government has allied
itself with a substantial interest apparently representing
a large constituency, the trade unions. It has shifted the
emphasis and the criterion of public policy from the

[4] Mr Bruce Page, Editor of the *New Statesman*, in a long article
(11 August, 1978) on a patient who obtained damages for
injury during surgery, discussed the legal aspects but neglected
to consider the relevance of the monopoly control of medicine
by th state.

production of values for the consumer and husbandry in government for the taxpayer to job preservation or job creation for the employee. It has transformed the ethos of industry from *adaptation* to change, or, as it used to be when Britain was the workshop of the world, *anticipation* of change, to *resistance* to change. That is a radical transformation that cannot be absorbed without severe economic indigestion, causing industrial ulcers (like British Leyland), possibly requiring surgery if unarrested.

The echoes of 17th-century guild protectionism, 19th-century syndicalism, and 20th-century corporativism are loud and clear. If the outcome were experimental employee co-operatives that proved themselves unprotected from competition by subsidies or guaranteed markets, as argued by Mr Peter Jay,[5] there would be little to lose and possibly some experience in new methods of industrial organisation to gain. But if these ventures began by being subsidised by the state and proceeded to envelop and control the state, as British trade unions have been doing, the end-result would be economic seizure. Living standards would fall, at first relatively to those of Europe and North America, and then absolutely. And, in its effort to maintain the fabric of British economy and society, government could be impelled to make its polity more exclusive, nationalistic, xenophobic. Economic protectionism, internal and external, might provoke civic repression: direction of labour, regulation of enterprise, conscription of capital, intensified exchange control, and restriction of emigration.

The second anxiety is less obvious but no less

[5] *Employment, Inflation and Politics,* Occasional Paper 46, IEA, 1976.

disquieting. The state is clearly tempted to channel research into ways of making the best use of the resources it can raise to finance its activities rather than into ways of replacing them by better systems that would undermine its power. It would not be surprising if the state were more interested in encouraging and financing research into perfecting comprehensive schools rather than into methods of strengthening parental influence, or into removing NHS waiting lists than into methods of raising funds for medical care that responded to public preferences, or into methods of making nationalised coal more suitable for power stations than into new fuels that might make it obsolete, or into high-speed nationalised trains than into battery-driven vehicles likely to be run by individual owners on toll-financed roads.

This, then, is the dilemma for economic thought and public policy. Once whole sectors of human activity are closed, can they be re-opened by argument? or will they require upheaval and "revolution"?

JUDGEMENT OF ACADEMICS AND PUBLIC MEN— AND A THIRD VIEW

In its 21st year it is therefore timely for the Institute to take stock of its growth from infancy to maturity and to look to the future. Accordingly it invited thinkers and observers from academia and public life to contribute their reflections on the consequences of "cumulative economic constriction". Six academics were sent a "preamble" (pp. xix-xxi): two historians (Professors W. H. Chaloner of Manchester University and Norman Gash of St. Andrews), a philosopher-economist

(Professor F. A. Hayek, formerly of the London School of Economics), an economist-historian (Professor R. M. Hartwell of Oxford), an econometrician (Professor Ivor F. Pearce of Southampton), and a sociologist (Professor Julius Gould of Nottingham). To obtain the judgement of philosophically-inclined public men, the preamble was sent to three Members of Parliament whose writings had indicated they were in advance—or in the van—of thinking in their Parties: Mr Nigel Lawson (Conservative), Mr Raymond Fletcher (Labour) and the Rt Hon Jo Grimond (Liberal).

At a late stage an edited and shortened version of a broadcast on Radio Clyde by the Duke of Edinburgh, which offered a unique third view from outside these two spheres, was added. (Acknowledgements are made on page 199.)

The two Founder Directors of the Institute add a Prologue and an Epilogue in which they give their personal views of trends as seen from within the Institute.

Professor Chaloner, an economic historian, opens with contrasting reflections on the differences between two climacterics in Europe: the bloodless English Revolution of 1688 and the bloody French Revolution of 1789 and their relationship to the theme of this book. Professor Gash, a political historian, doubts whether the British party system will be able to reflect and apply public opinion on the emerging closed society.

Professor Hayek offers as his contribution a statement of his solution to the task of enabling government to resist pressure for arbitrary, indiscriminate benefits from group interests that is, in turn, undermining public faith in the ideal of democracy. He would divide

sovereign representative power into two democratic assemblies, or some better device, to enable the people at
large to reassert the supremacy of institutions that serve
the general will rather than group interests. He has been
developing this theme in his three-volume *Law,
Legislation and Liberty*,[6] and the most convenient recent
statement of it was an article in the March 1978 number
of *Encounter*, the editor of which is thanked for his
permission to include the revised and retitled version
here (the first and last paragraphs were, also, added for
this version).

Professor Hartwell analyses the "traps" of intellectual, bureaucratic, governmental, and political vested
interest from which he thinks it is possible to escape and
indicates how the escapes can be organised.

Professor Pearce, the econometrician aware of the
weakness of Keynesian econometrics, argues there is a
dawning recognition that government cannot protect
the people from reality and that it cannot bring Utopia
by detailed regulation of economic life.

Professor Gould sees reason for hope that the resistance of the self-preserving interests will be overcome by
improving public understanding of the consequences of
collectivisation.

The three uncommon public men contribute uncom-
monly thoughtful essays that, in various ways, indicate
disquiet ahead of their political coadjutors.

Mr Lawson, the Conservative who sits for a country
town, argues that the state has increased its power
because its advocates have claimed the moral superiority

---

[6] Vol. 1, *Rules and Order*, 1973; Vol. 2, *The Mirage of Social
Justice*, 1977; Vol. 3, *The Political Order of a Free Society*,
(forthcoming), Routledge and Kegan Paul.

of "public" over private activity, and because the supporters of the market have concentrated on its economic beneficence and political advantages, which the public regards as less important. He therefore believes the danger of an *impasse* between the anxiety for reform away from state domination and the resistance to reform can be resolved by public re-education because the moral case for voluntary exchange in the market is stronger than for coercion in a state economy.

Mr Fletcher, who sits for a mining constituency, is in advance of the Labour Party, or one large wing of it, in sensing a desire among working-class Labour supporters to keep more of their earnings to spend by personal choice and to see the "social wage" gradually phased out. And, in addressing his Labour confrères and supporters, he envisages the three obstacles—the political demagogues, the administrators of the "social wage", and the trade unions—being overcome by reason and persuasion to show that all the people will benefit after the initial teething troubles. He tells the Labour Party it would not lose its supporters if it did what they *now* want, even if very different from what it thought they wanted 30 years ago; moreover, it will lose them if it does not. (This opinion is further illustrated in the Prologue.)

Mr Grimond, the Liberal, is less hopeful that discussion and persuasion will suffice. He argues that government may be reaching a point of no return in which suppression of individual freedom to work and invest would require a dictatorship to maintain even low living standards. The market has been distorted by pressure groups that can use political means to twist it in their favour, by the effect of high taxes in stimulating large size in industry, and by restrictive practices in trade unions and professional organisations. He advocates a "counter-civil service" to protect the people *against* the bureaucracy, vested interests, government, the establishment. Short of these measures he argues the corporate state and dictatorship may have arrived by 1984.

HRH Prince Philip outlines in his broadcast how he sees the world in AD 2000. (He emphasises that he describes what he thinks might happen, not what he would like to see happen.)

*   *   *

This collection of essays differs from other publications of the Institute in attempting to envisage the world ahead in which it may have to work: in which the economic approach it developed in two decades and several hundred studies will be either adopted (or adapted) or neglected by the vested interests generated by state economy that will understandably, but not less objectionably, resist them. The authors have spoken freely, and with evident candour, of the dangers they see ahead. Differences among the 12 contributors will be apparent. Their views are not necessarily shared by the Institute's Trustees or Advisers.

The Institute hopes the collection will provide a vivid text to stimulate thinking among teachers and students of economics, political science and history on the long-term consequences of alternative policies that politicians subjected to short-term pressures may be tempted to ignore.

October 1978   Editor

PREAMBLE

"For how long can an open society be closed by cumulative restrictions before it becomes difficult to 're-open'?

"If the restrictions create expectations of permanence of employment, incomes and other property rights, will proposals for reform by analysis, debate and persuasion encounter tension and discord with a risk to the survival of liberal society?

"Which policies of constriction have gone too far?

"Which remedies are required to repeal or reverse them?

"British political parties have introduced (or acquiesced in) cumulative restrictions ranging from the restraints on independent activity in fuel and transport, education and medical care to the most recent controls on prices, incomes and profits and legalised (trade union) inhibitions in the press and broadcasting. In activities not directly controlled by government it restricts independent initiative by regulation, standards, requirements, taxation and other indirect controls.

"In the coming years the restrictions may continue not because of their benefits but because the thinking that supports them and the occupational interests they have generated will resist reform despite change in conditions that made them outdated and damaging. The resistance is understandable; the fundamental question is whether yielding to it is compatible with the continuance of open society.

"The tendency to a modern form of 17th-century guild system or to a 20th-century corporate state may be imperceptible. Beyond a stage it may be too late to discuss what can be done by gradual liberal reform. The time to consider the possible *impasse* is therefore now, in 1978, before the restrictions have solidified, and while it is still possible to anticipate the consequences and to hope that reasoned and informed debate can check or reverse the restrictions by increasing public awareness of their consequences.

"The scope for independent initiatives in industry, commerce, civic and cultural life in Britain has been constricted for three peace-time decades since World War II, and in origins for a century or more. Each constriction could be urged plausibly on grounds of day-to-day urgency or expediency to deal with human suffering from poverty, unemployment, poor housing, ill-health, inaccessible education, or similar conditions. Each time the long-term consequences could not be (or were not) taken into account. Yet the acts of government have left a legacy of consequences that are borne in following decades by succeeding generations.

"Will liberal society continue if the long-term consequences are not built into day-to-day policies designed to meet immediate circumstances? Is it inevitable that the consequences must be neglected or ignored in policy-making?

"The essays will discuss (*a*) whether such an *impasse* can be envisaged that would become too difficult to prevent, at least by debate and discussion, (*b*) whether it seems far distant or imminent, and (*c*) what measures can be taken in good time to avoid it.

"The essays will enjoin judgement rather than prophecy. 1989 seems far enough off to leave room for reflective introspection but soon enough to suggest that re-thinking may be advisable in the near future. George Orwell's *1984* may be alarmist; but AD 2000 may be too late. 1989 is the middle date."

January 1978 R.H./A.S.

CHANGE BY DEGREE OR BY CONVULSION

Arthur Seldon

The Author

ARTHUR SELDON was born in London in 1916, educated at Raine's Foundation School and graduated from the London School of Economics, where he was Research Assistant to Sir Arnold Plant, 1937-40. He was a Tutor in Economics for the London University Commerce Degree Bureau, 1946-56, and a Staff Examiner in Economics to the University, 1956-66.

After editing a retail journal and advising in the brewing industry, he joined the Institute and wrote its first *Paper* in 1957 (on pensions), its early reports on advertising, hire purchase and welfare with Ralph Harris, and several later *Papers*. His essay, "Remove the Financing Flaw in 'Public' Services", was published in *Catch '76 . . .?* He is co-author, with Ralph Harris, of *Pricing or Taxing?* and *Not from Benevolence . . . .*

He wrote *The Great Pensions Swindle* (Tom Stacey, 1970), and compiled *Everyman's Dictionary of Economics* with the late F. G. Pennance (J. M. Dent, Second Edition 1976). He wrote *Charge* for Maurice Temple Smith, 1977. He has been an occasional contributor to the *Economist*, the *Financial Times*, *The Times* and the *Daily Telegraph*.

Change by Degree or by Convulsion

The form in which change takes place, and therefore the intensity of the resistance to it, depends on its rate. Here is perhaps the most fundamental distinction between the market and government. In a functioning market with monopoly bottlenecks minimised and access to supply widened by topping up low incomes, decisions in adapting supply to demand are decentralised to individual undertakings or establishments— factories and shops, mines and docks, schools and hospitals. Change is organic, gradual, continuous, by degree. It affects relatively small numbers. Disturbance, dislocation, disruption are minimised. The "confrontations" in the market are small, and solved by higgling and haggling over price, the peace-maker.

In a state economy or state industries, decisions are centralised to planning boards, committees, commissions, councils, government departments, that nominally "represent" the very much larger number of workers, managers and consumers who will benefit or suffer. Change is therefore more likely to be opposed, repressed, inhibited, postponed. When it takes place it is contrived, jerky, discontinuous, lumpy, convulsive. Disturbance, dislocation, disruption are large-scale. Friction is inflated.

In a market there are therefore better prospects that

change will be peaceful. In a government economy change is more likely to provoke tension, strife, and unrest, and, if it is suppressed, violence, bloodshed and civil war.

Since the end of World War II the British economy has become more and more resistant to change, and therefore more prone to discontinuous, "disruptive" change. The central government solidified the growing structure of variegated health services into "the" National Health Service, education into standardised schools, transport and fuel into nationalised organisations. Reorganisation, as in the NHS, cannot now come more often than, say, at 15-year intervals. Regional and local government has enlarged its activities, and made them more inflexible and "brittle". Government supplies more or less monopolised services. And, far from their mystical role as "public" services making the attitude of their trade unions more sensitive to the wants of the public, their economic power to pass on high wage costs in high consumer prices has made them more vulnerable to the pressures of trade unions.

It is thus hardly surprising that, not least in the two personally most sensitive state services, education and medical care, adaptation and reform are thwarted by the trade unions, or at least by the officialdom that claims to speak for the rank and file. Even local experiments in reform, such as the education voucher in Kent, or small-scale variations, such as the 1 per cent of beds for which patients sacrifice other comforts to pay for privacy or informal contact with family, are opposed or openly defied by the trade unions, or by officials who regard the "public" services as private preserves.

Yet it is misleading to blame the unions, and certainly

misguided to condemn working people. Most union activities, even if sometimes bereft of brotherly idealism, rest on two sources of power, both created by government: the trade union law as passed by Conservative, Labour and Liberal governments in 1875, 1906, 1946 and 1975, and the market power created by nationalisation in fuel and transport, by the welfare state in education and medical care, and by the more recent expansion of local government services.

THE UNIONS, THE LAW AND STATE-CREATED MONOPOLY

It is not so much trade union members that should be blamed, nor even the officials that lead them, even though often elected by derisory minorities. To adapt Shakespeare: as long as the law allows it, and the artificial state monopoly awards it, the trade unions will not surprisingly exert their power. Nor is there refuge in the amiable tendency to personify the power politics of trade union bargaining: to suppose that, if only (say) Mr David Basnett or Mr Moss Evans or Mr Clive Jenkins could be made to "see sense", all would be well. If "seeing sense" means settling for a lower wage than the state monopoly makes possible and the law allows the unions to enforce by strike-threat, picketing, immunity from action for damages, etc., the authority of the officials would be undermined by shop-stewards or others prepared to promise a harder line—as when incomes policies have widened the gap between approved and competitive pay. History and analysis indicate that the effective way to help Messrs Basnett *et al* to "see sense", and retain the adherence of their members, is to repeal the privilege clauses of the 1906,

1946 and other Acts and to denationalise the state monopolies.

"CONFRONTATION" OR APPEASEMENT

The risk as seen by some in the press, Parliament and industry, is "confrontation" with the unions. Is "confrontation" inevitable? Or is there a choice of "confrontations"?

The delicate question is whether continuing appeasement of a growing power outside Parliament, yet created or tolerated by government and the law, is permissible if it prevents the adaptation of the British economy to underlying changes in the conditions of supply and demand, a consequence especially debilitating for a country that has to export a fifth of her domestic product to maintain her living standards and her influence in the world.

Business men, politicians and journalists anxious to maintain social peace look to incomes policy as a means of avoiding "confrontation". Scarcity of resources impels man to make the best use of them. In so doing he must make difficult choices: in allocating resources of men, capital, land or money to some uses he must deny them to others. In a free society based on a market economy the "confrontations" take place on a small scale between buyers and sellers. And the differences are resolved by compromising on price. The larger the units of buyers and sellers, the larger the "confrontation", and the larger the risks to civil peace. And at the other extreme to the market, in the state economy, the "confrontations" are massive, since they are the outcome of power exercised by a handful of men over masses of other men.

There are thus two aspects of confrontation that should be clear. The first, and more immediate, is that appeasement brings only a short "peace". The choice is between little confrontations that ruffle tempers and big confrontations that risk social strife. The longer the "confrontation" is shirked, the more the paper tiger is pumped up into a bullfrog. The power of the trade unions does not lie so much in the power-hunger of trade union officials as in the failure to change the trade union law or to denationalise state monopolies—despite public opinion that would support both policies.

The second aspect is even more fundamental. The open society cannot long survive a power created or tolerated by Parliament that is invited to bargain with government. Down the centuries the British have disciplined the regional barons, the divine right of kings (bloodlessly in 1688 before it was too late, as the French found in 1789), the political church, the landowners, the House of Lords, monopoly business. The longer the disarmament of the monopoly unions is shirked, the more painful it will have to be. Even now it may be too late to disarm it without friction, as in the combative flying pickets of 1972 and the violent picketing at Grunwick of 1977. The unions, perhaps unjustly, are being seen for the first time among ordinary people, not least "working-class" wives, as engines of tyranny. Their tyrannical power to destroy the open society by repressing open debate is frighteningly illustrated in the reluctance of seven publishers to accept a book because, the author thought about several of them, it might upset the printers.[1] (Two said as much.) If the unions can prevent

[1] Sir John Colville, 'Dryden and the Guilty Men', *Sunday Times*, 6 August, 1978.

the publication of opinions they (or a handful of officials) dislike, Orwell's *1984* may not be long delayed. To suppress this consequence of continued appeasement is not to avoid confrontation but, by encouraging or misleading the unions, to provoke it.

Two important corollaries follow. First, those who wish to change society by revolution will resist small confrontations in the hope of building up steam for a disruptive "confrontation". Second, those who say "no confrontation" either knowingly promote or unknowingly acquiesce in the increasingly state-dominated post-war economy that creates tensions, discords, frictions, and larger confrontations by its incursion into private lives.

"PUBLIC" GOODS AND SOCIAL CONFLICT

Why has the scope for conflict been widened by government action and, less obviously but no less harmfully, inaction? Such are the issues—the role and function of government in causing *avoidable* social friction—that have been, not surprisingly, ignored by politicians and, more surprisingly, by social and political scientists. The unnecessary encroachment of the state into the provision of non-public goods, which it must decide by the only process it can use—the majority procedures of "representative" machinery—has created tensions by the resentment of more and more individuals that their lives are *unnecessarily* subjected to irrelevant and prejudiced political and politicised procedures.

It has long been argued by sociologists, typified by the late Richard Titmuss, and by some economists that social cohesion required the provision by government of common goods and services—education, medical care and others—to be jointly shared and used by individuals who would thus feel more securely bound to one another as members of a society. Conversely, individual activities that diverged or deviated from the common behaviour, not least private education and medical care, were regarded as creating "social divisiveness" and were therefore objectionable. This was, at root, the moralistic/sociological rationale for (comprehensive) state education and the National Health Service, to which access was to be equal and unrestrained, and for the Welfare State in general. It is an ethos that still pervades all political parties. The more convincing explanation of social "divisiveness" is virtually the opposite: that, except in "public goods", the supply by government of monopoly or near-monopoly services from which there is no escape by people they do not satisfy destroys social cohesion and creates social divisiveness.

The claim of the state to provide the citizenry with indispensable goods and services is strongest in "public" goods. In a sentence, the term describes defence, law and order, public health protection against contagious disease and other such goods that must be provided by government (or other collective associations) and paid for by compulsory taxes "voluntarily" agreed (or rather decided by majority or other fraction less less than 100 per cent) because they cannot be refused to people who refuse to pay.[2] These services must be

[2] Technical accounts of "public goods" are in Maurice Peston, *Public Goods and the Public Sector,* Macmillan, 1972, and C. K. Rowley and A. T. Peacock, *Welfare Economics,* Martin Robertson, 1974. A simple short discussion is in A. Seldon, *Charge,* Maurice Temple Smith, 1977.

supplied (or organised) by government or not at all. Government is not efficient at supplying them, since it cannot know individual preferences. It is almost certainly true that it does violence to individual wishes: thus the state may decide on 6 per cent of GNP as the optimum proportion to spend on defence, but individual preferences may vary from the pacifists' or Russophiles' 0 per cent to the Russophobes' 10 per cent. And much the same may be true of all other public goods. (A first attempt to measure the spread is made by the IEA in a new field survey in 1978.) But at least government has the reason of necessity for supplying public goods, and there is a general public sense that no other method is as feasible or convenient.

The issues are very different with non-public goods which do not have to be supplied by government at all. The arbitrariness, inequities, crudities and very rough justice in the decisions on the nature, scale and disposition of public goods are magnified many times in the use of the same political or committee majority machinery for non-public goods or services. Here is the genesis of potential social conflict in British society and elsewhere. Why?

Most of the activities of British government, national and local, are of this kind. It produces goods (coal, water, etc.) and services (transport, education, medical care, housing, libraries, fire services, job centres, refuse collection, even some police services, and many others) that it does not have to supply. And it does so by the same necessarily coercive machinery of committees of one kind or another ruled by majorities as for "public" goods. Moreover, the people sense it. That is the source of much of the incipient social tension, friction and conflict, which will intensify the more such services government supplies and the longer it supplies them.

There are various forms of social conflict generated by the sense that services are imposed on individuals by the unnecessary political coercion of other individuals who happen to have, or have had, the control of the machinery of government by temporary majority (or even *minority*). The forms of politically-created conflict are numerous; among them are:

1. *Regional/national:* the Scots may think the more numerous English and Welsh in Westminster decide their education, medical care, many other services (and the taxes to pay for them); so may the Welsh about the English and Scots.

2. *Sectarian/religious:* the Northern Irish Catholics are subjected to unnecessary coercion by the majority of Protestants who use the political process to decide their education, housing and other aspects of their private lives.

3. *Racial/religious:* coloured immigrants (and white minorities) are needlessly coerced into having their children educated in state schools designed by white, Protestant majorities. Pakistanis may wish their daughters to be taught in single-sex schools, Catholics in Catholic schools. All must pay taxes for schools decided by "representative" machinery in which they are out-voted.

4. *Fiscal/entrepreneurial:* the minority of risk-takers, innovators, the exceptionally talented (in art, culture, sport, etc.) and the highly skilled are

coerced by the progressive taxation voted by the majority of security-seekers, non-innovators, modestly talented, medium- or low-skilled.

5. *Employment-status:* the minority of independent-spirited self-employed are coerced by legislation (on employment security, etc.) prejudicial to small-scale traders, professional advisers, etc. (and their employees) passed to appease the majorities employed by large-scale units.

6. *Occupational:* majorities of established doctors, actuaries, lawyers, architects, printers, engineers, dockers, etc., legally coerce minorities of new entrants by acting as judge and jury in prescribing unnecessarily costly training, apprenticeship, superfluous staffing, demarcation or other protective devices.

7. *Familial:* minorities of parents, children and other relatives are legally coerced by political majorities into paying for medical care, education and other services they do not want, and are then virtually compelled by financial pressure to use them.

8. *Urbs in rure:* the activities of minority countrymen (fox-hunting, etc.) are inhibited or prohibited by laws enacted by "representatives" of town-dweller electoral majorities.

9. *Bureaucratic:* the minority of 4 million government employees, from teachers to messengers, exercise their influence over transient, amateur, pliant politicians to coerce the majority of private employees into paying for the unnecessary security

of tenure, over-manning, inflation-proofed pensions, concealed leisure in working time, "eating for the Queen",[3] excessive holidays of "public" (government) employees, and to pay for protected employment in relatively inefficient, high-cost, nationalised fuel, transport, education, medical care, or municipalised airports, libraries, refuse-collection, slaughterhouses, etc.

10. *Committee-government:* minorities of adroit, articulate activists use the committee machinery that controls state services (schools, hospitals, medical services, local authority services) to coerce majorities of maladroit, inarticulate inactivists.

11. *Sexual:* majorities of politically-minded men make national laws and local bye-laws that coerce majorities of domestically-inclined women.

12. *Elitist (reverse discrimination):* minorities of would-be do-gooder élitists coerce the majority of pre-occupied citizens by preferment of minority-group individuals (poor, immigrant, coloured, etc.) over better-qualified majority-group individuals.[4]

13. *Cultural:* minorities of cultural élitists claiming "social benefits" use taxes to coerce the "uncultured" majority into financing minority arts: working-class soccer-goers subsidise middle-class opera-goers.

[3] Professor Alan Peacock, in *The Economics of Politics*, Readings 18, IEA, 1978.

[4] A young London woman, who found immigrants lower down the list preferentially rehoused, asked "Does my British birthright count for nothing?"

14. *Patrician:* the majority of viewers and listeners is unnecessarily coerced, and denied technically possible choice, by a tiny minority of "the great and the good", from Beveridge to Annan, that have advised continuing the artificial government control of broadcasting channels.

15. *Monopolistic:* trade unions are empowered by law to coerce the minority who would have obtained employment at lower pay by forcing (by threat of strike, etc.) higher pay for the majority of existing members.

REPRESENTATIVE OR UNREPRESENTATIVE GOVERNMENT?

Students of "representative" democracy may observe that the advance of government beyond the realm of public goods and their invasion of the private domain makes democracy *unrepresentative*. In public goods, where economists are working on refinements of voting rules and electoral procedures,[5] voting machinery normally rests on majorities of one kind or another and coercion of minorities is unavoidable. (Quixotic voting systems may enable minorities to coerce majorities, as in the UK since 1945.) But in the provision of private benefits it is impossible to accept that the principle of "one-man-one-vote" applies to the machinery of elections, committees, boards of (school) governors, area

[5] Professor Gordon Tullock, a Founding Father of the economics of politics, discusses electoral machinery and other elements in "the theory of public choice" in *The Vote Motive,* Hobart Paperback 9, IEA, 1976. More advanced discussion of "social welfare functions" is indicated by Professor Duncan Black in "On Arrow's Impossibility Theorem", *The Journal of Law and Economics,* The University of Chicago, 1969.

health councils, and other nominally "representative" bodies that are supposed to reflect the opinion of total constituencies or populations. This machinery gives *more* than one vote to people who can organise and lobby and manage the machine, and *less* than one vote to individuals who lack these faculties, devices, skills and crafts. The advocate of massive or extended state control of services providing private benefits characteristically defends his case by claiming that the machinery is "representative" of, and accountable to, those who are intended to be benefited. In practice the claim cannot be substantiated. This is one more egalitarian myth.

REACTION FROM COERCED INDIVIDUALS/FAMILIES

Most of these tensions and potential conflicts derive from stubborn use of political machinery to provide non-public goods that could be supplied to individual taste or family requirements in the market, and thus with little or no coercion of minorities. The tension will intensify in the coming five, ten or twenty years as public understanding of the *unnecessary* coercion to which individuals have been subjected in their intimate personal and family lives goes beyond resentment to rejection. For a century or more the British (and other peoples) have been induced by politicians into believing that government must supply not only the ("public") goods and services that only it can supply, and in which they therefore had to accept group majority or national decisions, but also a long and lengthening list of goods and services that the politicians insisted voters were not competent to decide for themselves as individuals or families (or smallish local, voluntary, "co-operative" groups). Their growing awareness of this political confidence-trick will be intensified by the reinforcement of their *anxiety* to exert individual preferences (to send a child to a school or hospital of the parents' choice, the most common examples so far), by the growing *ability* to exert the choice made possible by growing incomes (or by drawing on saving, or by mothers working). And the more their aspirations are thwarted by political insensitivity, bureaucratic obstruction or trade union resistance, the stronger the resentment will grow and the more strenuous the reaction will be. "Confrontation" is intensified by coercive representative majorities that invade private lives.

The six forms of reaction by coerced citizens have been analysed by Professor Charles Rowley[6] as "instruments of political participation": voting (for example, by "senior citizens"), pressure groups (junior doctors), social movements (leading, if unsatisfied, to civil disobedience by dispossessed professional groups), individual economic adjustment (tax avoidance leading to evasion,[7] leisure, malingering, do-it-yourself activities), revolution (or more likely *coups d'état* by small groups which avoid giving "free rides" to non-rebels), and emigration ("voting with one's feet") analysed in the relatively new economic theory of clubs.[8] There are examples in this book of all six reactions.

RECOGNITION BY POLITICAL PARTIES
There are indications that the possibility of growing

[6] *The State of Taxation,* Readings 16, IEA, 1977, pp. 69-72.
[7] Discussed in *Tax Avoision,* a forthcoming IEA Readings.
[8] Charles Rowley, "Taxing in an International Labour Market", in *The State of Taxation, op. cit.,* pp. 73-4.

reaction will be recognised in time. In all three political
parties there is awakening anxiety about the subjection
of the individual by the state. The contributions in this
book from the three public men indicate anxieties that
must be shared by others in their parties and could
grow in time to obviate stronger reaction from individual citizens. Such development would not be surprising in the Conservative and Liberal Parties, although
both have legacies of paternalism, benign or authoritarian. A Labour reaction against the state and in
favour of the individual may be more surprising, but
could be all the more significant. A new organisation,
Mutual Aid Centre, formed by Lord (Michael) Young,
a veteran Labour Party adviser, and Dr Eric Midwinter
of the National Consumer Council, is important both
for its scepticism about the beneficence of the state and
for its proposals of voluntary, co-operative activities. It
creates a new approach sharply contrasted with the
étatism that Labour has espoused since it was created
in 1900.

A significant symptom of an emerging common
approach among people in all three Parties is the
interest in the education voucher, which is itself a tocsin
that distinguishes those who approach policy-making
through the state and through the individual. The
Conservatives have taken the initiative in encouraging
Kent County Council to initiate experimentation,
Liberals have discussed a pressure group to promote the
idea, and Labour intellectuals have been working on a
"left-wing" version of a voucher. How far the impetus to
create more effective parent-power has come from
thinker-politicians and how far from dissatisfaction
among parents will be for historians to judge. What

seems clear is that Labour will have to decide, perhaps in the coming ten years, before 1989, whether it sides with "the workers" in education (and medical care and elsewhere), as represented or misrepresented by trade union officials, or with its historic constituency of working-class parents (and patients) growing out of their proletarian origins and increasingly able to pay school fees, health insurance premiums and mortgage instalments. "The workers" are "trading up", and the politicians will not suppress them.

Among Labour protestors at the inquisition or persecution by tax-gatherers of small-scale traders is a much respected Labour elder statesman, and an authority on the tax system. The necessary consequence of high taxation is the increasing powers of tax-inspectors to pursue taxpayers by new powers of entry (if necessary, by breaking into homes or offices), described by Lord (Douglas) Houghton as "the thin end of the wedge".[9]

"There is no justification for the prevailing philosophy among income tax men that they are entitled to parity of powers of forcible entry with the excise men . . . if evasion is increasing, as it probably is, may the cause be that direct taxation in conditions of inflation and falling real standards have something to do with it?

". . . if so, the new power to . . . demand documents and the right to break-in . . . is not part of the battle against evasion so much as part of the counter-attack upon the resentful mood of the people. And I mean the people.

"The taxmen . . . are not noted for their interest in any civil liberties except their own . . . they are not the best judges of the politics of taxation."

[9] *The Times,* 16 August, 1976.

The flavour of these remarks re-appeared in an address by Lord Houghton to an IEA Seminar in 1977.[10]

FORMS OF PROTEST

A further consequential danger should be emphasised. Professor Rowley's "social movements" have appeared for some years in demonstrations, marches, sit-ins, and other forms of dramatised protest by parents (at William Tyndale School) and by people with more arguable causes—council tenants, hospital workers, students, and others. Democratic representative politicians and governments heed such activities both because they are ostensibly representative (at least of the articulate and the activist) and because they are noisy. Yet there is no more justice in yielding to noisy protests than to un-noisy resentment. The deeper-lying danger is that it teaches the normally quiet citizen that only noise wins attention. The argument was once put to a Labour Home Secretary: "If you yield only to those who march, you will induce ordinary people to take to the streets." That is what comes of destroying markets in which the individual citizen can "protest" by withdrawing his purchasing power and, without distressing confrontations, moving quietly to a preferred supplier. Or will historians in the 1990s record accelerating skirmishes for good and bad causes? If they do, the blame will lie with those who prevented change by degree in the market.

THE MARKET, "PLANNED ECONOMY" AND DIRECTION OF LABOUR

The logic of this analysis will be unpalatable to those who, possibly for the best of reasons, have looked to the

[10] *The State of Taxation, op. cit.*, pp. 51-63.

state as the guarantor of distributive justice and democratic liberties. Lady (Barbara) Wootton persists in her belief over 40 years that only the state in "democratic socialism" can yield these fruits. I have long owed her a debt of gratitude since, as an undergraduate at the London School of Economics in the 1930s, I first learned from her *Plan or No Plan*[11] the massive superiority of the market ("no plan") over central direction of the economy ("plan"), even though her book was intended to teach the opposite. 40 years later she sticks to her guns in the best response she can muster[12] to the challenge to show where in the world civil liberties are respected in a socialist economy. The challenge, she affirms, is "easily met": what has not yet happened (that a socialist state so far *has* respected civil liberties) may yet happen (because rapid technical and social change will make them possible, or more likely). But neither has she demonstrated the opposite: that what *has* happened (no market: no civil liberty) will not recur. The onus of evidence is on her. For she is asking us to abandon the market, which *has* yielded personal liberties, for a non-market economy which, she agrees, has not "as yet permitted the political and civil freedoms now enjoyed by the British". The opponents of the market have thus abandoned confident assertion of the superiority of the state for defensive claims that, as a matter of faith, "checks and balances" will preserve basic liberties, although how or why is not explained.

Lady Wootton concedes that centralised planning may require direction of labour. Even more interesting is

[11] Gollancz, 1934.

[12] "Can we still be Democratic Socialists?: Why we need a Planned Economy", *New Statesman*, 4 August, 1978.

her new conclusion that, after all, markets have a useful role to play—as taught in the Yugoslav "self-regulating" enterprises or workers' co-operatives and the Hungarian shift from administrative order (central planning) to control by incentives (market devices).

Lady Wootton as economist at last sees the essence of the market—that it *dispenses* with autocratic or paternalistic central planning (and its built-in tensions and antagonisms). That new insight is still hidden from central planners who are not economists. Yet she and they still hanker after a dream-world of good men (and in these days we must add women) who will know enough of the people's individual preferences to be able to direct resources to serve them faithfully and efficiently. Economists until recently allowed political scientists such a lot of rope in pursuing the will-o'-the-wisp of men transformed into benefactors on election to "public" power or selection for "public" office that they have almost hanged themselves intellectually. The economists may yet save them by extending economics from the study of industry in the market with all its much-mulled-over imperfections to the study of politics (without markets) and all its long-neglected imperfections.[13] I suspect political scientists will be learning more from economists in the next few years about the working of political government than economists have learnt from political scientists about the working of the market.

CONSERVING INSTITUTIONS OR PRINCIPLES

A parallel dilemma faces those at the other extreme of the philosophic spectrum who so fear the uncertainties

[13] *The Economics of Politics, op. cit.*

of reform that, like Sir Ian Gilmour,[14] Mr William Waldegrave[15] and Mr Maurice Cowling,[16] they look to continuity, tradition and custom to safeguard the civilised values of society. This approach would preserve established institutions but risk loss of the purposes and principles they were erected to serve. They would preserve practices of which they do not approve, like trade union and professional closed shops and other legal immunities and privileges, because sanctified by usage. But they make the same mistake as the opponents of "confrontation": by opposing small-scale reform in the market they do not avoid change but make it more discontinuous, and thus risk the very continuity they hope to preserve.

LONG-TERM ECONOMIC CONSEQUENCES OF POLITICAL ACTS

Such are the long-term consequences of short-term policies that the essays in this book are intended to explore. They indicate that much or most of the thinking in the last 30 years—and further back for about a century—will have to be abandoned. It offered *short*-term solutions to immediate problems—poverty, unemployment, inflation, inequality in education, medical care and housing, sluggish rates of economic growth—but at a cost in *long*-term effects for which no politician or government will accept the blame but which our children, our grandchildren and our country will suffer: unemployment, inflation, failure to keep pace not

[14] *Inside Right,* Hutchinson, 1977.

[15] *The Binding of Leviathan: Conservatism and the Future,* Hamish Hamilton, 1978.

[16] *Conservative Essays,* Cassell, 1978.

only with our neighbours and the rest of the world but, even worse, with our own past, so that Britain must be denied the improvements that could come from the advance of science and influence in world affairs.

REASONS FOR HOPE

Yet there are five reasons for hope. The most immediate and elemental is the growing resistance of the family to invasion by the state. The family is the protector of private lives that the state invades at its peril. Resistance will come in the two most intensely personal services wrongly provided by the state: medical care and education. When parents are prevented from spending their money on a kidney machine to save their child's life and fathers are prepared to be imprisoned rather than see their children sent to schools decided by officials to suit the system, it cannot be long before politicians see that state medicine and schooling will require intensifying coercion that the British people will increasingly resist. Tax-evasion will be accompanied by state-evasion. Unless the state introduces tax credits or vouchers, by which all who feel oppressed can escape, only the better off or self-sacrificing who pay (taxes) for services they do not use as well as (prices) for services they prefer will be able to escape. And, as incomes rise, there will be no way to stop the increasing number from escaping, short of destroying the open society. Instead of creating equality of access, the state therefore will have created inequality of exit. The egalitarians are surprisingly slow to see this development. Yet it is possible to envisage a growing demand by families for private medical care and education better than the state can provide equally for all out of taxation.

The market could satisfy that demand; only the state could suppress it. Yet the egalitarians again do not see the potential social conflict in the "confrontation" of new private aspirations and state standardisation.

Second, the resistance of the family will be reinforced by the approaching equality and the emerging influence of woman. As wife, mother and daughter (and to a lesser degree as a less close relative) she will prefer markets to governments. She does the household as well as the personal buying, she shops around, she compares prices, she knows the power over the shop-keeper of the ability to shop elsewhere by taking her purchasing power with her. In her wish to do the best for her family she is more concerned than man with take-home pay that she spends than with the social wage that others spend for her. She is less exposed than man to accept mass decisions, or moral pressure, in factory, trade union, or political meetings. She feels herself less a member of a group or a class than an individual. She has less concern about social cohesion than about family well-being. She is less moved by abstract notions than by everyday realities. In short, she is unconsciously more than man in favour of the market and more frustrated than man by the coercive majority machinery of public choice that prevents her from doing what she does best. Rising incomes will reinforce her micro-attitudes. By now micro-woman would have laughed out of court, and destroyed by derision, the schoolboy pretensions of macro-man to run complex industrialised society by a coterie of élitists. That may be why the matriarchal society of America is based on the market and the patriarchal society of Russia tries to run itself from the centre. And that is why emerging micro-woman in Britain will increasingly assert the family against the state.[17]

It is probably, moreover, the "working-class" wife, armed with new purchasing power to buy "middle-class" comforts, not least when her children want them most, who will reject the burgeoning welfare state and its high taxation that reduces her husband's take-home pay. It is from the lower but rising income groups, therefore, that the rejection of the state in favour of the market is the more likely. The visitor to market-orientated Japan, Taiwan and Hong Kong can have little doubt where the preferences of emerging peoples will lie. In the 19th century the market replaced state regulation despite what John Stuart Mill called "The Subjection of Women." In the 20th century the market could be all the more strengthened by the assertion of woman.

Third, government will find it more difficult to raise revenue because of the growing anxiety about the corrupting effects of high and rising taxes. The "tax revolt" in Britain began long before the Referendum on Proposition 13 in California. The revolt has been accelerating; and politicians in all parties are recognising it. Mr Callaghan has said "[people] want less tax and more money in their pockets". There is little reason to suppose they will "want" higher taxes at any time in the future.

They are resisting it by what might be called tax "avoision", an unconscious rejection of the moral difference between legal avoidance and illegal evasion,

---

[17] Fortunately micro-woman is more numerous than macro-woman who, like macro-man, claims to know how other people should live and would compel them by majority rules.

that is spreading in all social classes. The difficulty of raising revenue may induce government to reserve for public goods the revenue it can raise, and to finance by varying forms of charging the wide array of separable private benefits it has been adding to its functions. Charging would not only raise revenue but also lead to a more rational allocation of functions by channelling private services to the market. If people have to pay out of pocket for state benefits formerly free or subsidised, they will prefer to pay for private service with more choice and authority over the supplier. The state sector will therefore be reduced to comprise essentially public goods.

Fourth, it cannot be much longer before intellectuals of all schools, not least with Labour sympathies, see that there was never a case for universal, all-embracing, exclusive, state medicine or schooling (or any private services). The most the advocates of the (supposed) benefits of state control could claim was a trial for a period in one region (or more) to demonstrate whether or not the hoped-for good results were likely to be reproduced on a national scale. But without a jot of evidence they introduced exclusive systems, and moreover resist criticism, comparison and reform. After 30 years of the NHS they assume or claim another 30 years to remove its defects.[18]

Even then there is a further hurdle to surmount. If the condition for the effectiveness of state medicine or education is the exclusion of all other systems to prevent

[18]An example in an otherwise acute observer is Professor Rudolf Klein: "Who Decides? Patterns of Authority", *British Medical Journal*, 1 July, 1978; and "An Unquestionable British Success", *The Times Higher Education Supplement*, 21 July, 1978.

creaming off, say, doctors or high-ability children, the lost opportunity of discovering better systems is too high a price to pay. I do not see how any political or social scientist can believe the contrary. This is at bottom the flaw of all exclusive systems, whatever compassionate labels they give themselves.

Moreover, there has never been a popular vote in favour of a *permanent* National Health Service or comprehensive state schooling. Until there are single-policy referenda (with price-tags for alternatives), no British government can claim a mandate for any of its policies, except on public goods. Public understanding of this confidence trick also is awakening.

Fifth, again except in public goods, the market finds its way back, or rather people find their way to it. Sixty years ago in a minor classic the Austrian economist Böhm-Bawerk[19] argued that political power would sooner or later succumb to economic law, the market. That is, politicians would have to defer to the people, who are uniquely enfranchised by it. Countries that have tried to suppress the market have had to restore it sooner or later, or suffer confusion or chaos. When they restore it, the rulers' power is shifted to "market forces", in other words, ordinary men and women; so they suppress it, until chaos returns. These countries have demonstrated by such alternations that in practice the alternative to the market is coercion. And that is why the British, who have seen the market increasingly suppressed or repressed, and can now judge the results,

---

[19] "Power or Economic Law?", 1914; reprinted in the *Shorter Classics of Böhm-Bawerk*, Libertarian Press (South Holland, Illinois, USA), 1962.

will want to restore it—not least in medicine and education, where it was said to be least practicable.

*   *   *

All this because we thought we could avoid the dis-
comforts of change by obstructing change itself. If this
is what people are thought to want, let them be told
the price. And let *them* make the choice. Until that
choice is explained and exercised, the suspicion must be
that those who stand by the state fear that the verdict
of the people will be peaceful change through the
market. The "confrontation" with truth, so long delayed
by unproved and untested hypotheses spuriously in-
vested with political authority, by the élitist preference
for "public" over private, and by unfounded fear of
inevitable and beneficial change, may come before or
after 1989. The sooner the better for the prospect of
preserving and strengthening the open society that
Britain gave the world by precept and example.

PART I

HISTORY

History

1989: 1688 OR 1789?

W. H. Chaloner

The Author

WILLIAM HENRY CHALONER was born in 1914 and educated at Crewe Grammar School and the University of Manchester where he has been Professor of Economic History since 1976; formerly Reader in Modern Economic History, 1962-76. From 1939 to 1945 he was in the Press Censorship Division of the Ministry of Information.

Professor Chaloner's publications include *Social and Economic Development of Crewe 1780-1923* (1950); *Vulcan Boiler 1859-1959: One Hundred Years of Engineering and Insurance* (1959); *People and Industries* (1963); (with R. C. Richardson) *British Economic and Social History* (1976); (with Barry Ratcliffe) *A French Sociologist Looks at Britain* (1977); and various translations, notably his collaboration with Dr W. O. Henderson on Engels. He has contributed articles to learned journals including *History Today, History, English Historical Review,* and *Economic History Review.* Hon. Ed., *Transactions* of the Lancashire and Cheshire Antiquarian Society. For the IEA he contributed an essay (with W. O. Henderson), 'Friedrich Engels and the England of the "Hungry Forties" ', in *The Long Debate on Poverty* (Readings 9, 1972; 2nd Edition, 1974).

1989: 1688 or 1789?

In 1989, no doubt, the French people and government will rightly commemorate the bicentenary of their French Revolution, as they celebrated its centenary in 1889. We know that in 1788 local, if not nation-wide, celebrations of England's Glorious Revolution of 1688-89 took place, but little or nothing was done to commemorate its bicentenary in 1888 (it was probably too soon after Queen Victoria's jubilee festivities of the previous year). Will there be enough enthusiasm and historical imagination to launch a commemoration of the tercentenary of the accession of William and Mary in 1988? The Revolution settlement is, after all, the nearest we have to a British constitution. Popular understanding of it should be fostered at a time when there is a sustained, if as yet somewhat unconcerted, attack on its principles. (Glorious has in recent years been written derogatorily as "Glorious", as though to cast doubt on the description.) What changes have occurred in the intellectual climate to damp down interest in the political upheavals of the late seventeenth century, once so beloved of British writers and politicians?

FROM GLORIOUS TO "GLORIOUS"
The answer is to be found in the seduction of our intellectuals, and particularly academic intellectuals, by

the radical appeal of the vague French ideals of liberty, equality and fraternity, and by the spread of Marxist ideas, fostered unwittingly by a tolerant State itself through the recent expansion of higher education and subsequent infiltration. The abstract and emotional principles of the French Revolution have never been received or adopted in Britain, which has its own traditions of freedom to set against "liberty". The pursuit of "equality" is a will-o'-the-wisp, in spite of the preachments of R. H. Tawney. As a Frenchman[1] put it, the spirit of equality is widespread among children and immature adults—while "fraternity", if not based on the family or the close association of the voluntary society or club, is nebulous nonsense.

Fortunately for British political progress and stability the Revolution of 1688-89 was bloodless, but instead of rejoicing, modern revolutionary intellectuals find it a cause for disappointment and suspicion, because it appears to disprove one of their favourite justifications for revolutionary violence and judicial murder: "you can't make omelettes without breaking eggs". Modern left-wing intellectuals have found consolation in their espousal of the so-called "English Revolution of 1640-60" (it used to be called the Puritan Revolution before radical scholars "went off religion", or adopted the new one of Marxism). This has been one of the fastest growth-points of historical research since the late 1930s and the heyday of the Left Book Club.

LOCKE AND "POSSESSIVE INDIVIDUALISM"

At the same time the Revolution Settlement of 1688-1714 and the Whig interpretation of history which held

[1] An eminent social and economic historian, in a private conversation with the writer.

sway for the following two hundred years have been under increasing criticism. (Professor Herbert Butterfield's *The Whig Interpretation of History*, which laid the debate open to popular interest for the first time in 1931, now seems rather thin and inadequate.) John Locke (1632-1704), once the revered political philosopher of the Williamite settlement, has now become the object of modern radical attack, and it is not difficult to see why. Locke was a stubborn defender of private property:

> "The great and chief end . . . of men's uniting into commonwealths, and putting themselves under government, is the preservation of their property."

Property, to which man had a natural right, was defined by Locke in a wide sense as 'life, liberty and estate'. How, without men of property and independent means, could private individuals stand up against the powerful State? This "doctrine of possessive individualism" is, of course, a dangerous doctrine in the opinion of our latter-day collectivists, who consider it to be subversive of the foundations of the Socialist state and an affront to doctrinaire egalitarianism. Hence their general reluctance to support the movement for a new Bill of Rights to serve as a fundamental guarantee of British freedoms, and to replace the Bill of Rights of 1689[2] which the passage of three centuries has now rendered inadequate to protect the liberties of the subject.

[2] In David Ogg's words, the Bill of Rights of 1689 "reaffirmed what had been asserted by the great medieval jurists, that the king (i.e. the executive) is subject to law; and that for many of his most important acts, there must be the consent of those (whether *magnates* or parliament) who could claim to speak on behalf of the nation". (*England in the Reigns of James II and* [*continued on page 36*]

Modern radical antipathy to the Glorious Revolution has now extended to the Hanoverian succession, Sir Robert Walpole and eighteenth-century Whiggery. The latest exponent of this hostility is Mr E. P. Thompson, who now sounds more like a Jacobite,[3] rather than the Jacobin[4] we all thought he was, in his harking back to a mythical Stuart paternalism. In a curious article in *The Times Literary Supplement* of 1973, followed by a full treatment in a book published two years later, he launched a furious denunciation of an Act of Parliament of 1723 passed against deer-stealers, cattle-maimers, armed gangs of poachers and vandals operating in the Royal Forests. It is little wonder that the latest historian of early Hanoverian England, Dr W. A. Speck, remarks:

> "The view that a ruling-class ideology found expression in laws to protect property is most tendentiously expressed in E. P. Thompson, *Whigs and Hunters: the Origin of the Black Act*."[5]

FROM PATERNALISM TO FREEDOM

The liberating influence of the ideas of philosophers such as John Locke and Bernard Mandeville and economists such as Sir James Steuart and Adam Smith

William III, 1965 edn., p. 243.) Ogg's short account of the Bill (pp. 241-5) should be supplemented by Jennifer Carter, "The Revolution and the Constitution", in G. Holmes (ed.), *Britain after the Glorious Revolution, 1689-1714,* Macmillan, 1969, pp. 39-58.

[3] "Alexander Pope and the Windsor Blacks", *The Times Literary Supplement*, 7 September, 1973, pp. 1,031-33.

[4] A reading of *The Making of the English Working Class* shows very clearly what our forefathers would have called his "Jacobinical" views.

[5] *Stability and Strife: England, 1714-1760,* Edward Arnold, 1978, p. 294.

during the eighteenth and early nineteenth centuries led directly and indirectly to the decline in the enforcement or in the legal abolition of many obsolete restrictions on free enterprise in economic life. These had for the most part been imposed during the so-called period of Tudor and Stuart paternalism, not so much because of sympathetic royal interest in "the condition-of-the-people question", as from a desire to foster the stability of the two dynasties by trying to remove possible causes of public riot and disorder. Examples of this type of restrictive legislation were the regulations affecting the internal wholesale trade in corn outside the public markets and between different areas of the kingdom, fixing statutory prices and weights for various sorts of bread (the Assize of Bread),[6] the cumbrous and ineffective county machinery for fixing, at Quarter Sessions, the maximum rates of wages in a variety of occupations (the Statute of Artificers, 1563), and the restrictions on the numbers and conditions of artisan apprenticeships. By the mid-1820s all these had not merely fallen into desuetude but had been swept away by Parliament.

Throughout the eighteenth century and particularly after the South Sea Bubble of 1719-20, monopolistic practices and enterprises tended to be looked upon by Parliament and public opinion with caution and grave suspicion. Long before 1800 foreign visitors had been marvelling at the remarkable freedom of British economic life, in comparison with the pettifogging systems of bureaucratic control which hampered businessmen and industrialists in, say, France, Russia

[6] W. Duncan Reekie, *Give Us This Day* . . ., Hobart Paper 79, IEA, 1978. The Assize of Bread involved the fixing of the price of bread and the sizes of loaves by the Justices of the Peace.

and Prussia. There can be little doubt that this atmosphere of economic freedom contributed to the rapid development and productive triumphs of the Industrial Revolution in Britain.

The espousal of French Revolutionary ideas by English poets, extremist dissenters and political publicists in the 1790s is richly documented, thanks to Tawney's friend P. A. Brown, whose book *The French Revolution in English History* (1918) has not yet been superseded, although increasingly inadequate. A considerable literature now exists on the subject, on the whole uncritically sympathetic to the mixed bag of idealists, fellow-travellers and crackpots whose "sufferings" have been lovingly researched by successive generations of scholars since the beginning of the 20th century. So the curious situation has developed that a large segment of the British intelligentsia sympathises with the conscious and unconscious dupes of authoritarian régimes against which successive British governments fought long, bloody, and ultimately successful wars between 1793 and 1815. British admirers of Napoleon continued to believe in the essential peacefulness of his aims and, what was more, the essential wickedness of the British Government, and to hamper the prosecution of the war right up to the news of Waterloo.

Like the radical disappointment with the bloodless character of the Revolution of 1688-89, a similar sense of disappointment can be traced in the writings of historians and others, who, taken with the violent character of the French and subsequent revolutions, seem to regret there was no bloody Jacobin revolution in Britain during the period 1790-1830, alleged to have witnessed "the making of the English working class". Reviewers have pointed out the unusual frequency with which the word "bloody" occurs in E. P. Thompson's *The Making of the English Working Class*, first published in 1963. This book has given birth to a host of disciples and would-be imitators. What does this new wave of revolutionary thinkers hope for the British state in the closing years of the twentieth century?

READING LIST

Sir H. Butterfield, *The Whig Interpretation of History*, (1931), Penguin, 1973.

C. B. Macpherson, *The Political Theory of Possessive Individualism: Hobbes to Locke*, O.U.P., 1964.

R. C. Richardson, *The Debate on the English Revolution*, Methuen, 1977.

David Ogg, *England in the Reigns of James II and William III*, O.U.P., 1955.

J. R. Jones, *The Revolution of 1688 in England*, Weidenfeld and Nicolson, 1972.

Maurice Ashley, *The Glorious Revolution of 1688*, Hodder & Stoughton, 1966.

G. Holmes (ed.), *Britain after the Glorious Revolution, 1689-1714*, Macmillan, 1969.

H. T. Dickinson, *Liberty and Property: political ideology in eighteenth-century Britain*, Weidenfeld & Nicolson, 1977.

J. H. Plumb, *The Growth of Political Stability in England, 1675-1725*, Macmillan, 1967.

W. A. Speck, *Stability and Strife: England, 1714-1760*, Edward Arnold, 1978.

E. T. Lean, *The Napoleonists: a study in political disaffection, 1760-1960*, O.U.P., 1970.

J. R. Western, *Monarchy and Revolution: the English State in the 1680s,* Weidenfeld & Nicolson, 1972.

History

THE BRITISH PARTY SYSTEM
AND THE CLOSED SOCIETY

Norman Gash

The Author

NORMAN GASH was born in 1912 and educated at Reading School and St John's College, Oxford, at which he was a scholar. He has taught history at the Universities of Edinburgh, London, Leeds and Oxford. Since 1965 he has been Professor of History at the University of St Andrews, where he has been appointed Dean of the Faculty of Arts until 1980. His main published works are *Politics in the Age of Peel* (1953); *Mr Secretary Peel* (1961); *Reaction and Reconstruction in English Politics, 1832-52* (1966); *The Age of Peel* (1968); *Sir Robert Peel* (1972); *Peel* (1976). For the IEA he wrote an essay, "The State of the Debate", for the 2nd Edition of *The Long Debate on Poverty* (Readings 9, 1974).

The British Party System
and the Closed Society

I

Political parties are based on history, ideas and interests: they organise private energies for public ends; they represent human nature in politics. For that reason few philosophers include a party system in their ideal political constitutions. The notion of paying one set of men to govern, and a second set of men to criticise, obstruct and if possible eject them from office, is not a rational one. Yet time and habit legitimise most things, and it is not difficult to construct a practical defence of the party system as it has grown up in Britain.

PURPOSE OF PARTIES

A party system keeps men in power wary and flexible; it replaces them when they grow tired with a fresh team, it relieves public discontents by offering alternative policies and leaders; it formulates issues and devises solutions. In a democratic constitution it provides the machinery whereby the government of the people can be carried on for the people—or as near to it as the diversity of human nature, the complexity of human affairs, and the defects of human institutions allow. In

43

short, a party system performs for the electors a task which they are unwilling or unable to perform for themselves. It makes democracy workable; and that is no inconsiderable achievement.

The traditional British view of the party system is apt to be based on two assumptions. The first is that the political instincts of the British people find their characteristic expression in a two-party system. If this means that two parties only have monopolised British parliamentary representation, it is patently untrue. Since 1832 it would be difficult to find a single year in which small parties have not existed beside the large. Radicals, Irish Nationalists, Peelites, Home Rulers, Liberal Unionists, the Scottish Crofters Party, the ILP, the pre-1914 Labour Party, the post-1922 Liberals, provide a continuous pattern of small parties existing long before the emergence of Scottish and Welsh Nationalists. Sometimes, as with the Peelites between 1846 and 1859, or the Home Rulers in 1885, a third party has held the balance of power. Even coalitions, though less frequent, have been a recurrent feature of British political history. The Napoleonic, the first and second world wars all produced coalition government; the Crimean War was unusual: it began with a coalition and ended with a single-party administration. Even in peace there have been coalitions: in 1852 and 1895, for example, as well as in 1931. Yet the popular assumption is sensible. Compared with many multi-party continental states, where coalition government is almost the rule, it remains true that the bias of the British system is towards two major parties, one of which at any given time is governing the country.

TWO-PARTY SYSTEM: ADVANTAGES

The bias is both historical and mechanical. The aristocratic dualism of Whigs and Tories was transmitted in the nineteenth century to the Victorian Liberal and Conservative parties. The electoral system in the half-century following the Reform Act of 1832, when the two-member constituency was the standard electoral unit and uncontested returns common, made no appreciable difference to the dominance of the two major parties. Nevertheless, the gradual adoption after 1885 of single-member constituencies, electing by a simple majority, constituted a further handicap for small parties. Until a considerable body of electoral support is built up, concentrated in specific areas rather than spread over the electorate as a whole, the voting support for minor parties is never adequately rewarded by parliamentary seats. The British electoral method favours large parties; exaggerates small shifts of opinion between them; and ensures that parliamentary strength reflects not the aggregate voting in the country but the cumulative total of individual constituency successes.

It is therefore notoriously possible for a party to win a majority of seats in the House of Commons without securing a majority of votes from the electorate. The working of the electoral system, though not necessarily the sentiments of the British electorate, accord with the biblical precept: to him that hath shall be given. The perennial difficulty of translating votes for minor parties into an equitable proportion of seats in turn reinforces the practical inclination of the electorate to vote for one or other of the two large parties. Many people do not care to cast a vote for a candidate who is unlikely to be elected or a party that cannot conceivably obtain office. There are powerful technical reasons why the British system is still in a broad sense essentially a two-party system. An alteration in electoral law might well effect a profound alteration in the structure of the party system.

II

Another popular assumption is less frequently challenged. It is that the two main parties which compete for the favours of the electorate differ fundamentally from each other in the policies they propose and that the intrinsic virtue of the system resides in the possession by the electorate of a choice of opposites. This is a fallacy. A successful party system rests on the axiom that the parties must agree on fundamentals and differ only in details.[1] It does not take much reflection to see why. There is a demonstrable advantage in having two teams of men who take turn and turn about in the exhausting work of governing the country. But unless there is a basic continuity in the work of successive administrations, the periodic changes of ministers incidental to a party system produce dislocation and confusion in the permanent institutions of the country. The wider the area of governmental action, the more damaging the effects of this discontinuity on society as a whole. It is one thing to sail the ship of state in a particular direction, changing the crews at regular intervals; it is a different matter to have the ship sailed

[1] [This convergence is discussed by Professor Gordon Tullock in *The Vote Motive,* Hobart Paperback 9, IEA, 1976.—ED.]

first in one direction and then in another because the rival crews disagree completely on their destination.[2]

COMMON ADHERENCE TO TRADITION; BUT CONCEALED REVOLUTION?

If in the past the stability of British government was admiringly contrasted with the brief and ineffective parliamentary ministries of many democratic European states, it was not merely because of the relative simplicity of a two-party system. It was also, perhaps more fundamentally, because of the underlying homogeneity of the British political tradition that allowed the party system to work with such little real friction. In continental states, where monarchist, legitimist, Bonapartist, clerical, radical and republican parties differed on the very nature of society and constitution, the success of one side or the other formed not a mere incident in the game of "ins" and "outs" but the victory of one incompatible faction over another. The consequences were often not so much a change of administration as a concealed revolution. There is nothing in party politics as such which makes politicians intrinsically moderate, tolerant and law-abiding. Though in nineteenth-century Europe political parties were the characteristic creation of middle-class societies, the feature of the first half of this century was the ease with which extreme movements—Fascist, Communist, National Socialist— adopted the respectable guise of a parliamentary "party" in order to secure a totalitarian régime which would bring the whole bourgeois "party system" to an

[2] [The effects of this common outlook on fundamentals in "opposing" parties in post-war Britain is also discussed in other essays.—ED.]

end. Where society is divided, demoralised and impoverished, men may come to believe passionately in a *party* but not in the tolerance and restraint necessary for a party *system*.

England itself experienced such a phase, though so long ago that this has been forgotten. The Whig and Tory parties emerged in the late-seventeenth century in the course of a bitter struggle over fundamental issues of government, the dynasty, and religion in which the penalties for failure were imprisonment, exile and the scaffold. Even the revolution of 1688 did not end this deadly party animosity. The consolidation of the Hanoverian dynasty after 1714 was only possible on the basis of one-party rule. The defeated Tories were systematically deprived of office and power in both central and local government; and the "Whig Ascendancy" lasted even after Walpole's retirement in 1742. Not until the accession of George III in 1760 were the Tories politically rehabilitated and the two warring factions of the later Stuart period transformed into a single governing oligarchy. But that reconciliation was only possible because the two Tory principles of Stuart legitimacy and Anglican supremacy had been quietly abandoned. Politicians had to agree on "Whig" fundamentals before a new party system could begin to emerge.

From the middle of the eighteenth century until 1830, however, the House of Commons was controlled by a homogeneous class of landed gentry who were divided into sets and factions, including a sizeable group of independents, rather than into two opposed, monolithic parties. It was not difficult in these circumstances for politicians to develop tolerant attitudes towards one another, or for the House itself to establish its significant reputation as the best club in Europe.

UNVINDICTIVE TRADITION

One of the most profound differences in practice between the nineteenth-century Westminster parliament and its continental counterparts lay in these aristocratic origins. The ethos of the Victorian party system was derived from the tolerant, sporting, unvindictive tradition of the landed gentry between 1760 and 1830. Aristocratic leadership persisted in politics and government long after it had lost its economic and intellectual dominance. The fundamental traditions of the House of Commons, formed when it was a closed assembly of peers' sons, gentry, service officers and lawyers, were transmitted without a break to the late-Victorian political parties based on the wealthy, educated middle-classes and a democratic mass electorate. Historically the party system that evolved after 1832 owed its success to the tacit readiness of the two main parties, cast in this aristocratic mould, to work within agreed limits. Successive administrations accepted most of the ordinary and all the fundamental legislation of their predecessors. The two front benches often seemed closer to each other than to their respective back benchers. Continuity of administrative problems and political pressures acting on responsible ministers tended to produce similar solutions.

PERMANENT ADMINISTRATION AND
IMPERMANENT MOODS

Though on the hustings the politicians emphasised their differences and laboured to persuade the electorate that

Codlin was the friend, not Short, in practice their conduct in office bore remarkable resemblances. General
elections took the place of the *coups d'état*, impeach-
ments, assassinations and revolutions of unhappier eras
and less fortunate societies. It was a civilised, sophisti-
cated method of operating a representative political
system and understandably received much praise, if not
always complete understanding. Only rarely between
1832 and 1914 did issues arise such as Home Rule in
1885-86, the reform of the House of Lords in 1909-11,
and Ulster in 1912-14, which threatened to cancel the
unwritten laws to which the main parties conformed.
For the most part the system maximised the *appearance*
but minimised the *reality* of political divergencies. It was
a remarkably efficient mechanism for making the continual adjustments necessary in any open society
between the permanent tasks of the executive and the
impermanent moods of the electorate.

III

Agreement on fundamentals, aided by the continuity
of the British political system over the last two and a
half centuries (a continuity unknown to any other leading political society in the world), had one further
consequence. It made not only possible but natural a
constitution in which there are singularly few restraints
on the sovereign power of the legislature.

UNWRITTEN CONSTITUTION: FEW RESTRAINTS
ON LEGISLATURE

Other countries, taught by tyranny, anarchy, war and
revolution, or suddenly emancipated from the rule of a

benevolent mother-country, have looked to written constitutions for the framework of their political life and
the guarantee of their liberties. In Britain the homogeneity of the governing classes, and the evolutionary nature
of the process whereby political power was gradually
conceded by the aristocracy to the whole community,
made such safeguards seem unnecessary. What is
generally meant by the "unwritten" nature of the
British constitution is little more than a combination of
conventions of parliamentary government and a virtual
absence of constitutional restraints on the exercise of
sovereign power by an executive based on a majority in
the legislature.[3]

The consequence has been a gradual but in the end
remarkable accumulation of power unaccompanied by
any serious attempt to lay down constitutional as
distinct from political limits to government action. The
"fundamental" clauses in the Acts of Union with
Scotland and Ireland were never legally more sacrosanct
than any other statutes, and were in the course of time
amended or repealed as their usefulness seemed ex-
hausted. The last statutory restrictions on the power of
the executive were applied between 1688 and 1714 and
were directed at the new foreign wearers of the Crown
—the Dutch William III and the German George I.
Otherwise the only important new constitutional
limitations have been the twentieth-century acts reducing the legislative powers of the House of Lords.

---

[3] [The significance of the constitution is discussed by Professor
Hayek and of rule by majority in the Prologue.—ED.]

BRITAIN RULED BY UNI-CAMERAL LEGISLATURE: MONARCHY AND LORDS NEUTRALISED

But these acts merely transferred authority within the legislature as a whole. Indeed, by concentrating more power in the House of Commons, the acts increased the power of the legislature. With the disuse of the crown veto, ultimate authority is now concentrated in one branch of the legislature, the Commons, rather than divided between all three. When the active assent of the three was necessary for legislation, there was a practical if not legal restraint on each and therefore collectively on all. That among other things was what was meant by "a balanced constitution"—a phrase which significantly has disappeared for over a century from British political vocabulary. Parliament today is a bi-cameral legislature in form rather than in substance.

IV

The modern British party system therefore is the product of historical circumstances and grew up in the way it did because it answered contemporary needs. It is not necessarily endowed with permanent or universal values; nor is it something the British people would necessarily perpetuate if circumstances changed.

PARTY SYSTEM COULD BE CHANGED

If it is encountering criticism today, however, it is not because of the multiplicity of small parties and the difficulty of obtaining stable parliamentary majorities. Those small parties are symptoms rather than causes of the malfunctioning of the political system. It is a situation which has occurred before and has been endured without undue damage to the political life of the country. The real problem is the enormous power enjoyed by one party when in command of the parliamentary machine, and the widening gap between the fundamental policies of the two major parties.[4] In the past, while possessing definable traditions and principles of their own, the governing parties shared a common outlook on the general purpose of government and nature of their society. Their differences were those of emphasis rather than of essence. The displacement of the Liberal Party by a doctrinaire Labour Party in the first quarter of this century changed that relationship. Sympathetically since 1906, formally since 1918, practically since 1945 the Labour Party has been identified with the full socialist policy of the nationalisation of the means of production, distribution and exchange with a consequential commitment to the vast extension of state direction necessary to secure those objectives. Since the end of the Second World War it has been in a position periodically to realise successive instalments of that programme and make even wider attempts to transform the nature of British society.

The significance of this development for the traditional system of party politics has been realised only slowly. The period of "Butskellism" represented both a common recognition of certain political tasks and a continuation on the Conservative side of the tradition of practical co-operation in national policy between the parties. The issue today, however, is no longer whether the two major parties can continue to retain any

[4] [The divergence is analysed by the "new" economics of politics: Tullock, *op. cit.*—ED.]

agreement on fundamentals. For one party it is whether anything can be done to arrest, if not reverse, the steady progress of British society towards a form of corporate state incompatible with its basic principles of personal liberty and a market economy. Unless party politics are to become a game of ins and outs, the Conservative Party is threatened with spiritual extinction. Literally construed, a conservative administration in a collectivist state could do no more than conserve collectivism; it would be an exercise in self-contradiction. The logical end of collectivism is a one-party state.

ASYMMETRY IN PARTY POLICIES

The nature of collectivist legislation makes a reversal of the collectivist process extremely difficult. As the history of the steel industry—nationalisation, denationalisation, renationalisation—demonstrated, contradictory policies applied to a complicated and sensitive branch of industry produce such disorganisation, inefficiency and loss of confidence that in the end assumption of financial responsibility by the state becomes the only solution. The ratchet effect of collectivist legislation makes an accomplice of every conservative administration. In the past the Conservative Party has prided itself on its pragmatic approach to government. But in a contest with creeping collectivism a purely pragmatic party is like a naked man in his shirt facing an armed opponent.

ELECTORAL CONTROL OVER TRANSIENT MAJORITIES

In these circumstances men have begun to look for other remedies. No stronger proof of the declining efficacy of the party-system could be found than this growing conviction that occasional victories at general elections are no longer sufficient. Since the advance of the corporate state will depend on the periodic installation in office of a collectivist government wielding the sovereign power entrusted to a victorious party by the constitution, one obvious safeguard is to limit that power. Various ways of doing this have been canvassed.

It has been argued that a system of proportional representation, by producing a mathematically "fairer" representation of all parties, might habitually produce a legislature in which no one party would ever have an absolute majority; all governments would have to depend on a coalition or on a chance aggregate of votes in parliament. But there are many systems of proportional representation. Not all, perhaps none, can be guaranteed to prevent any one party from ever gaining an absolute majority. Moreover, whatever the British public might want, almost certainly the main political parties themselves are likely to prefer a system which produces strong, stable and unified administrations to one which is likely to result in less stable, less unified, less united governments. "England", said Disraeli on one occasion, "does not love coalitions". What he meant was that politicians do not love coalitions. Since any reconstruction of the electoral machinery would require the support of at least one of the two large parties, proportional representation in parliament hardly seems an immediate possibility; and the circumstances in which one of those parties could be brought to implement it are not easy to visualise.

Another suggestion has been the creation of legal and constitutional checks on the unrestrained use of

sovereign power. These could take different forms: a
Bill of Rights, a second chamber with entrenched
powers, a category of reserved legislation that would
require more than a simple majority vote, the use of the
referendum. It would not be difficult to devise a series
of reforms which would provide tangible safeguards
without unduly damaging the ability of government to
carry on the normal administration of the country. The
difficulty would lie in inducing the political parties, or
at least the Labour Party, to accept constitutional
limitations on its freedom of action when in office.

CONSTITUTIONAL CONTROLS

It is argued, not unreasonably, that no legal barriers
can long survive if there is no wish on the part of a
substantial section of the community to retain them.
Law in the last resort can only be an expression of the
will of society. One might go further and say that no
written constitution, no fundamental law, will be proof
against the determination of even one major political
party to overthrow a system of restraints to which it
never gave its assent. There is force in this argument;
but perhaps it can be carried too far. 'In the last resort'
is not the normal basis of political action. The law and
the constitution must ultimately reflect the settled ideas
and desires of society; but this is no reason for rejecting
what advantage can be derived from them at any given
time. Law is not simply a temporary expression of the
public will; it is also a social discipline in itself. Indeed
it is probably the most powerful social discipline of all:
a framework of rights, duties and sanctions which can
by their mere existence help to foster social conventions
and practices. Experience of other countries suggests

that constitutional and legal limitations are capable of restraining those who wish to go beyond but are reluctant to break the law. Not all radicals are revolutionaries.

The luxury of an unwritten constitution and of a party system in which parties are periodically entrusted with legally unlimited power has in the past been tolerable, even positively useful. But this was when the users of that power were in broad agreement on the nature and values of their society. In an age when the traditions and institutions of a free society are being ceaselessly undermined, it becomes a real question whether that luxury can still be afforded and whether those institutions should not only be defended but reinforced by means which would entail a diminution of the power enjoyed by a party in office. Even a holding action may be valuable.

There is no certainty that the public as a whole wishes to become the obedient population of a corporate state; or if they do, that they will not change their mind when they have had experience of its full rigours. The internal contradictions of socialism—the promise of better living and the practical inefficiency of its economy, the ideals of liberty and equality set against the reality of bureaucratic control, the autonomy of trade unions clashing with the growing power of the state—may yet produce a political reaction. In the end, if the British people want a corporate state, no doubt they will get it. If they do not react in time against collectivism, they may still get it. But these are propositions which have not yet been verified.

The task is to prevent a collectivist state arriving by default. Legal restraints may help; but in the end hard political facts will decide. Whatever the outcome it is difficult to see how the party political system can be continued on its present basis. Sooner or later one or other of the two major parties will have to abandon its fundamentalist assumptions.

PART II

ECONOMICS AND SOCIOLOGY

Economics and Sociology

WILL THE DEMOCRATIC IDEAL PREVAIL?*

F. A. Hayek

*[We are grateful to the editor of *Encounter* for permission to publish this revised version of an article which first appeared in the issue of March 1978. — ED.]

The Author

FRIEDRICH AUGUST HAYEK, Dr Jur, Dr Sc. Pol. (Vienna), DSc. (Econ.) (London), Visiting Professor at the University of Salzburg, Austria, 1970-74. Lecturer in Economics at the University of Vienna, 1929-31. Tooke Professor of Economic Science and Statistics, University of London, 1931-50. Professor of Social and Moral Science, University of Chicago, 1950-62. Professor of Economics, University of Freiburg i.Brg., West Germany, 1962-68. He was awarded the Nobel Prize for Economic Science, 1974.

Professor Hayek's most important publications include *Prices and Production* (1931), *Monetary Theory and the Trade Cycle* (1933), *The Pure Theory of Capital* (1941), *The Road to Serfdom* (1944), *Individualism and Economic Order* (1948), *The Counter-Revolution of Science* (1952), *The Constitution of Liberty* (1960), *Studies in Philosophy, Politics and Economics* (1967), *Law, Legislation and Liberty* (3 vols., 1973, 1976 and 1979), and *New Studies in Philosophy, Politics, Economics and the History of Ideas* (1978).

The IEA has published his *The Confusion of Language in Political Thought* (1968), *Economic Freedom and Representative Government* (1973), *A Tiger by the Tail* (1972, 2nd Edition 1978), an essay in *Verdict on Rent Control* (1972), *Full Employment at Any Price?* (1975), *Choice in Currency: A Way to Stop Inflation* (1976), and *Denationalisation of Money* (1976, 2nd Edition 1978).

Will the Democratic Ideal Prevail?

I interpret the question we are trying to answer in this collection of essays as: How long can government continue to increase its powers over the economy without harmful long-term consequences that would be difficult to check or to reverse by the procedures of democracy? My answer is to analyse the working of the democratic process as it becomes exposed to the importunities of pressure groups. This analysis is a short statement of the diagnosis on which I have been working for some years.

It is no longer possible to ignore that more and more thoughtful and well-meaning people are slowly losing their faith in what was to them once the inspiring ideal of democracy.

This is happening at the same time as, and in part perhaps in consequence of, a constant extension of the field to which the principle of democracy is being applied. But the growing doubts are clearly not confined to these obvious abuses of a political ideal: they concern its true core. Most of those who are disturbed by their loss of trust in a hope which has long guided them, wisely keep their mouths shut. But my alarm about this state makes me speak out.

It seems to me that the disillusionment which so many experience is not due to a failure of the principle of democracy as such but to our having tried it the wrong way. It is because I am anxious to rescue the true ideal from the miscredit into which it is falling that I am trying to find out the mistake we made and how we can prevent the bad consequences we have observed of democratic procedure.

A ''BARGAINING'' DEMOCRACY

To avoid disappointment, of course, any ideal has to be approached in a sober spirit. In the case of democracy in particular we must not forget that the word refers solely to a particular method of government. It meant originally no more than a certain procedure for arriving at political decisions, and tells us nothing about what the aims of government ought to be. Yet as the only method of peaceful change of government which men have yet discovered it is nevertheless precious and worth fighting for.

Yet it is not difficult to see why the outcome of the democratic process in its present form must bitterly disappoint those who believed in the principle that government should be guided by the opinion of the majority.

Though some still claim this is now the case, it is too obviously not true to deceive observant persons. Never, indeed, in the whole of history were governments so much under the necessity of satisfying the particular wishes of numerous special interests as is true of governments today. Critics of present democracy like to speak of "mass-democracy". But if democratic government were really bound to what the masses agreed upon there would be little to object to. The cause of the complaints is not that the governments serve an agreed opinion of the majority, but that they are bound to serve the several interests of a conglomerate of numerous groups. It is at least conceivable, though unlikely, that an autocratic government will exercise self-restraint; but an omnipotent democratic government simply cannot do so. If its powers are not limited, it simply cannot confine itself to serving the agreed views of the majority of the electorate. It will be forced to bring together and keep together a majority by satisfying the demands of a multitude of special interests, each of which will consent to the special benefits granted to other groups only at the price of their own special interests being equally considered. Such a bargaining democracy has nothing to do with the conceptions used to justify the principle of democracy.

THE PLAYBALL OF GROUP INTERESTS

When I speak here of the necessity of democratic government being limited, or more briefly of limited democracy, I do not, of course, mean that the part of government conducted democratically should be limited, but that *all* government, especially if democratic, should be limited. The reason is that democratic government, if nominally omnipotent, becomes as a result exceedingly weak, the playball of all the separate interests it has to satisfy to secure majority support.

How has the situation come about?

For two centuries, from the end of absolute monarchy to the rise of unlimited democracy, the great aim of constitutional government had been to limit all governmental powers. The chief principles gradually established to prevent all arbitrary exercise of power were the separation of powers, the rule or sovereignty of law, government under the law, the distinction between private and public law, and the rules of judicial procedure. They all served to define and limit the conditions under which any coercion of individuals was admissible. Coercion was thought to be justified only in the general interest. And only coercion according to uniform rules equally applicable to all was thought to be in the general interest.

All these great liberal principles were given second rank and were half forgotten when it came to be believed that democratic control of government made unnecessary any other safeguards against the arbitrary use of power. The old principles were not so much forgotten as their traditional verbal expression deprived of meaning by a gradual change of the key words used in them. The most important of the crucial terms on which the meaning of the classical formulae of liberal constitutionalism turned was the term "*Law*"; and all the old principles lost their significance as the content of this term was changed.

LAWS *v.* DIRECTIONS

To the founders of constitutionalism the term "Law" had had a very precise narrow meaning. Only from limiting government by law in this sense was the protection of individual liberty expected. The philosophers of law in the 19th century finally defined it as rules regulating the conduct of persons towards others, applicable to an unknown number of future instances and containing prohibitions delimiting (but of course not specifying) the boundaries of the protected domain of all persons and organised groups.

After long discussions, in which the German jurisprudents in particular had at last elaborated this definition of what they called "law in the material sense", it was in the end suddenly abandoned for what now must seem an almost comic objection. Under this definition the rules of a constitution would not be law in the material sense.

They are, of course, not rules of conduct but rules for the organisation of government, and like all public law are apt to change frequently while private (and criminal) law can last.

Law was meant to prevent unjust conduct. Justice referred to principles equally applicable to all and was contrasted to all specific commands or privileges referring to particular individuals and groups. But who still believes today, as James Madison could two hundred years ago, that the House of Representatives would be unable to make any "law which will not have its full operation on themselves and their friends, as well as the great mass of society"?

What happened with the apparent victory of the democratic ideal was that the power of laying down laws and the governmental power of issuing directions were placed into the hands of the same assemblies. The effect of this was necessarily that the supreme governmental authority became free to give itself currently whatever laws helped it best to achieve the particular purposes of the moment. But it necessarily meant the end of the principle of government *under* the law. While it was reasonable enough to demand that not only legislation proper but also governmental measures should be determined by democratic procedure, placing both powers into the hands of the same assembly (or assemblies) meant in effect return to unlimited government.

It also invalidated the original belief that a democracy, because it had to obey the majority, could do only what was in the general interest. That would have been true of a body which could give only *general* laws or decide on issues of truly *general* interest. But it is not only *not* true but outright *impossible* for a body which has unlimited powers and must use them to buy the votes of particular interests, including those of some small groups or even powerful individuals. Such a body, which does not owe its authority to demonstrating its belief in the justice of its decisions by committing itself to general rules, is constantly under the necessity of rewarding the support by the different groups by special advantages conceded to them.

LAWS AND ARBITRARY GOVERNMENT

The result of this development was not merely that government was no longer under the law. It also brought it about that the concept of law itself lost its meaning. The so-called legislature was no longer (as John Locke had thought it should be) confined to giving laws in the sense of general rules. *Everything* the "legislature" resolved came to be called "law", and it was no longer called "legislature" because it gave laws, but "laws" became the name for everything which emanated from the "legislature". The hallowed term "law" thus lost all its old meaning, and it became the name for the commands of what the fathers of constitutionalism would have called arbitrary government. Government became the main business of "legislature" and legislation subsidiary to it.

The term "arbitrary" no less lost its classical meaning. The word had meant "rule-less" or determined by particular will rather than according to recognised rules. In this true sense even the decision of an autocratic ruler may be lawful, and the decision of a democratic majority entirely arbitrary. Even Rousseau, who is chiefly responsible for bringing into political usage the unfortunate conception of "will", understood at least occasionally that, to be just, this will must be *general in intent*. But the decisions of the majorities in contemporary legislative assemblies need not, of course, have that attribute. Anything goes, so long as it increases the number of votes supporting governmental measures.

An omnipotent sovereign parliament, not confined to laying down general rules, means that we have an arbitrary government. What is worse, a government which cannot, even if it wished, obey any principles, but must maintain itself by handing out special favours to particular groups. It must *buy* its authority by discrimination. Unfortunately the British Parliament which had been the model for most representative institutions also introduced the idea of the sovereignty (i.e. omnipotence) of Parliament. But the sovereignty of the law and the sovereignty of an unlimited Parliament are irreconcilable. Yet today, when Mr Enoch Powell claims that "a Bill of Rights is incompatible with the free constitution of this country", Mr Callaghan hastens to assure him that he understands that and agrees with Mr Powell.[1]

[1] House of Commons, 17 May, 1977. There would in fact be no need for a catalogue of protected rights, but merely of the single restriction of all governmental power that no coercion was permissible except to enforce obedience to laws as defined before. That would include all the recognised fundamental rights and more.

It turns out that the Americans two hundred years ago were right and an almighty Parliament means the death of the freedom of the individual. Apparently a free constitution no longer means the freedom of the individual but *a licence to the majority in Parliament to act as arbitrarily as it pleases*. We can either have a free Parliament or a free people. Personal freedom requires that all authority is restrained by long-run principles which the opinion of the people approves.

FROM UNEQUAL TREATMENT TO ARBITRARINESS

It took some time for those consequences of unlimited democracy to show themselves.

For a while the traditions developed during the period of liberal constitutionalism continued to operate as a restraint on the extent of governmental power. Wherever these forms of democracy were imitated in parts of the world where no such traditions existed, they invariably, of course, soon broke down. But in the countries with longer experience with representative government the traditional barriers to arbitrary use of power were at first penetrated from entirely benevolent motives. Discrimination to assist the least fortunate did not seem to be discrimination. (More recently we even invented the nonsense word "underprivileged" to conceal this.) But in order to put into a more equal material position people who are inevitably very different in many of the conditions on which their worldly success depends, it is necessary to treat them unequally.

Yet to break the principle of *equal treatment under the law* even for charity's sake inevitably opened the floodgates to arbitrariness. To disguise it the pretence of the formula of "social justice" was resorted to;

nobody knows precisely what it means, but for that very reason it served as the magic wand which broke down all barriers to partial measures. Dispensing gratuities at the expense of somebody else *who cannot be readily identified* became the most attractive way of buying majority support. But a parliament or government which becomes a charitable institution thereby becomes exposed to irresistible blackmail. And it soon ceases to be the "deserts" but becomes exclusively the "political necessity" that determines which groups are to be favoured at general expense.

This legalised corruption is not the fault of the politicians; they cannot avoid it if they are to gain positions in which they can do any good. It becomes a built-in feature of any system in which majority support authorises special measures assuaging particular discontents. Both a legislature confined to laying down general rules and a governmental agency which can use coercion only to enforce general rules that it cannot change can resist such pressure; an omnipotent assembly can not. Deprived of all power of discretionary coercion, government might, of course, still discriminate in rendering services—but this would be less harmful and could be more easily prevented. But once central government possesses no power of discriminatory coercion, most services could be and probably should be delegated to regional or local corporations competing for inhabitants by providing better services at lower costs.

SEPARATION OF POWERS TO PREVENT UNLIMITED GOVERNMENT

It seems clear that a nominally unlimited ("sovereign") representative assembly must be progressively driven into a steady and unlimited extension of the powers of government. It appears equally clear that this can be prevented only by dividing the supreme power between two distinct democratically elected assemblies, i.e. by applying the principle of the separation of powers on the highest level.

Two such distinct assemblies would, of course, have to be differently composed if the *legislative* one is to represent the *opinion* of the people about which sorts of government actions are just and which are not, and the other, *governmental* assembly were to be guided by the *will* of the people on the particular measures to be taken within the frame of rules laid down by the first. For this second task—which has been the main occupation of existing parliaments—their practices and organisation have become well adapted, especially with their organisation on party lines which is indeed indispensable for conducting government.

But it was not without reason that the great political thinkers of the 18th century were without exception deeply distrustful of party divisions in a true legislature. It can hardly be denied that the existing parliaments are largely unfit for legislation proper. They have neither the time nor the right to approach it.

I have on various occasions sketched a possible organisation for such a democratic legislature and hope soon to publish a full account of it.[2] This plan, which I have worked out over many years, is, however, unquestionably only one way in which the aim can be

---

[2] See Chapters 7, 8 and 10 of my *New Studies in Philosophy, Politics, Economics and the History of Ideas* (Routledge & Kegan Paul, London, 1978), and the forthcoming third volume of my *Law, Legislation and Liberty*.

achieved. Here I am concerned solely with the general principle on which I have no remaining doubts: the absolute necessity of dividing in some manner the supreme power between two different and mutually wholly independent democratic assemblies with entirely distinct and sharply separated functions.

A reform of the House of Lords might offer an opportunity for a move in that direction.

If this solution of dividing supreme power into two independent democratic assemblies, or some better device, is not applied in the next 10 years or so, the public loss of faith in the ideal of democracy itself will continue to evaporate, especially if government acquires even more power over economic life and even more power to dispense arbitrary, discriminate benefits to group interests, that will, in turn, therefore, be increasingly disposed to organise pressure on it. The end-result must be either the collapse of political democracy or a renewed recognition by the majority, which suffers from such sectional favours, to re-assert the supremacy of institutions that serve the general will.

Economics and Sociology

TOWARDS A CHANGE OF COURSE

Julius Gould

The Author

(SAMUEL) JULIUS GOULD was born in 1924 and educated at Balliol College, Oxford. He has taught sociology at the Universities of London, California and Cornell. Since 1964 he has been Professor of Sociology at the University of Nottingham, where he is now Dean of the Faculty of Law and Social Sciences. He has been a member of the UK National Commission for UNESCO, and of the Sociology Committee of the SSRC. He edited (with W. L. Kolb) *A Dictionary of the Social Sciences* (1964); *Penguin Survey of Social Science* (1964); *Penguin Social Sciences Survey* (1968). Author of *The Rational Society* (1971); *The Attack on Higher Education* (1977).

Towards a Change of Course

Prophecies of doom—anti-utopias of all kinds—may be highly counter-productive. Cassandras, notoriously, are seldom well-received; but where their predictions are heeded (even subliminally) they can, to some measure, be self-fulfilling.

This effect is especially likely if it is claimed (or "proved") that a society is in the grip of remorseless "fundamental" forces: or that it is run by people who claim (or "possess") scientific insights into the nature of those forces and into the reasons for their being "fundamental". I do not believe there are "iron laws", in economics or sociology or in the burgeoning sciences of the environment. So when I see tendencies in contemporary Britain that I regard as destructive not of some abstract "status quo" but of the fundamentals of an open, democratic and energetic society, I do not sit back in despair. For those tendencies—even some of the tendencies praised as "irreversible"—have not come about by "necessity". They are not the outcrop of uncontrollable forces. They have come about because rulers and ruled, for nearly half a century, have been guided by (and in turn have moulded) certain social values and priorities.

These values, such as "welfare" and "equality", have an entirely admirable basis in human needs and aspira-

77

tions. But they steadily require interpretation—both in the abstract and in the concrete. And there is much scope for bias in such interpretation. Even more scope exists when it is claimed that *one* interpretation (only partially valid when first produced) is an eternal guide to social and political policy under later and entirely different conditions. The collectivist mock-liberal Establishment (not only in Britain) is aware of the constant need for re-interpretation. Hard-headed (and power-hungry) as its leaders are, they see they must re-interpret their myths. For such an exercise means an extension and widening of their political bridgehead, not a basis for a critical review of old, tedious or tattered assumptions. Such re-interpretations provide ready employment for the cultural employees, praise-singers and associates of that Establishment. They are acute enough to detect (often accurately) that there are logical flaws in, for example, an "ultra-"liberal economic analysis; they are vigilant to show when and where a "monetarist" devil mistakes an abstract model for a complex social and economic system. Yet they are ready enough to commit quite comparable, or even identical, sins.

FROM EQUALITY OF OPPORTUNITY TO EQUALITY OF OUTCOMES

A good example is the way in which in recent years the debate over equality has been shifted, both here and in the USA, from a concern with equality of opportunity to a concern with equality of conditions and outcomes. Equality of opportunity is not enough. For, in the words of the introduction to the Open University book of sociological readings, *Schooling and Capitalism*:

"The idea of equality of opportunity, the drive to establish a meritocracy based upon ability, while compensating those deprived of opportunity to participate in the movement towards upward social mobility, are shown neither to threaten nor to replace the essential economic structures of society."[1]

One way forward for modern theorists is to justify the reduction or elimination of the *unequal results* that the older doctrine justifies "on the basis of natural abilities and talents".[2] This is clearly a more ambitious task, requiring more dedication, ingenuity or ruthlessness on the part of the equalisers.

The intellectual (and indeed the social) origins of this shift are complex. But the *new ethos* (and its political usefulness) can be simply illustrated. First, the shift is based upon a distorted, often hostile, review of the "drawbacks" of equality of opportunity—a review that has led in Britain to the virtual elimination of excellent but academically selective grammar schools. (Among those who fostered this elimination, from their well-paid political and cultural positions, many were themselves the products of the much-derided equality of opportunity. They displayed intense pleasure in kicking down the social ladder by which they had ascended.)

Secondly, the new equality insists, *a priori*, on the

---

[1] *Schooling and Capitalism*, edited by R. Dale and others, Routledge and Kegan Paul in association with the Open University, 1976, p. 3.

[2] This is a reference to the views of John Rawls (footnote 4 below) in the discussion by Daniel Bell: *The Coming of Post-Industrial Society*, Heinemann, 1974, p. 441. Bell noted that the new principle of equality "has become linked with the principle of quota representation" (*ibid.*, p. 445). There are some keen British enthusiasts for such a linkage, suitably adapted to British conditions.

significance of equality (re-interpreted as equality of outcomes), at best neglecting and at worst despising both the parallel claims of liberty (not merely of an "abstract" economic liberty) and those issues that arise in rewarding individual merit, desert or excellence.

The problems in analysing liberty are no less difficult than those which concern equality (or, for that matter, fraternity). But it is an intellectual as well as a moral error (however politically attractive it may seem) to argue, or even imply, that equality *is* liberty, that extremism in the defence of equality is no vice, and that regardless of specific conditions or circumstances the drive for equality (*as* liberty . . .) is of paramount importance. Few of the progressive discourses on equality even mention the links between envy and equality, or that *fear of envy* arouses guilt feelings among the privileged, not least in Anglo-Saxon societies.[3] Collectivist politicians, unlike their intellectual allies, are clearly aware of this factor: and, with some success, they spread the thought that what cannot (for whatever reason) be readily made available to *everyone* is a source of dubious, self-seeking and indefensible "privilege". They often exempt themselves and their lifestyles from the full rigour of this thinking: but their hypocrisy is as unblushing as it is unyielding.

ENCOURAGING DIFFERENCES IMPORTANT FOR THE INDIVIDUAL AND SOCIETY

On the issues of encouraging distinctions (important differences of significance to the individual and to society) much too can be said. Such differences are of

[3] The classic and much neglected text is *Envy* by Helmut Schoeck, published in English translation by Secker and Warburg, 1969.

the highest value to any society that seeks to maintain its creativity—whether in technology or the arts. The majestic principle found in the most elaborate and most widely discussed recent book on equality—that of the Harvard Professor, John Rawls—proclaims, to quote from one of his gentler critics, that inequalities can only be justified "if and only if they are to the long-term benefit of the least favoured members of society".[4]

Logical and empirical difficulties would arise in applying this lofty notion. Obviously it cannot be a complete guide to public policy. The "most favoured" (by talent or inheritance or accident) are not a homogeneous category: some are more meritorious in some senses than others and some, quite conceivably, could have special claims for special (i.e. unequal) treatment. The same is sadly, indeed tragically, true of the "least favoured". The claims of the sick or the old or the disabled or of the wretched inhabitants of overcrowded jails are real, important and conflicting. But some persons (not any one principle) have to decide, in a world of scarcity (artificially heightened by monopoly and restrictive practices), on the allocation of resources to these, and other, categories of the unfortunate. Equal division of resources and rewards notoriously erodes differentials. And while much is unclear about the impact of differentials there is growing and justified concern about the impact of narrowed differentials upon productivity and output.

If the intellectuals affect to ignore these matters (except when their own position is threatened . . .) the

[4] Review of John Rawls, *A Theory of Justice* (Harvard University Press, 1971) by Charles Frankel in *Commentary*, September 1973, p. 54 *et seq.*

toolmakers of the British Leyland company constantly remind us that differentials are not the concern only of fat, cigar-smoking capitalists who desert the board-room for the golf-course. But the arguments over differ-ences extend beyond the confines or obsessions of incomes policy. They go to the root of a society's being —and its future. Small wonder there is a reaction (and not reactionary) from what Professor Ralf Dahrendorf in his Reith Lectures in 1974 called "the alienation of enlightened reason". He insisted that "equality is there for people to be different and not for the differences to be levelled and abolished". Small wonder too that many of us show a preference for an active constitution of liberty over the spurious "higher freedoms"; that we value individual choice (not the monopoly "freedoms" of organised labour and capital) over and above the fashionable perversions of equality. The cry of justice, central to the socialist creed and not confined to, let alone invented by, 19th-century Marxists, has led to frozen and ossified social forms. Professor Dahrendorf observed that

> "A century of socialist demands and pressures and appeals has in fact raised the common floor for all citizens very considerably. It has also lowered the ceilings and sometimes locked the doors and barred the windows so that people are safer but not necessarily freer."[5]

He is only one of several observers to point out how organised labour and capital have a joint common interest in making others pay for their obsessions, greed

---

[5] R. Dahrendorf, *The New Liberty*, Routledge and Kegan Paul, 1975. This passage is adapted from my review of the book, and its wider context, in *The Times Literary Supplement*, 8 August, 1975.

and myopia. Others, of course, regard the corporatism to which it points as a small price to pay for the realisation of egalitarian fantasies in the social field.

"PUBLIC" SERVICE BUREAUCRACIES: THE "FALSEHOOD EXPLOSION"

Third, the exponents of the new equality have helped to create the mammoth "public" service bureaucracies of our time—an exercise that has enhanced both their status and their incomes. Interestingly, the growth of state power has its obverse in what is known as "the permissive society". To cite an American student of these matters, Professor Robert Nisbet,[6] "There are after all certain freedoms which are like circuses". All too often this masks the curtailment of other more central freedoms. What is more, the expanded polity raises expectations that are unrealistic—which indeed no polity can meet: thus it alienates important groups. Too much is expected of the state and assumed by its agents. The disillusion that follows such *hubris* is fed by the growth of what Nisbet calls "organised, institutionalised lying in government". Nisbet was writing of the USA: and *perhaps* he overstated his case. I myself know of no way to measure the increase of mendacity among political leaders. But the phenomenon is not unknown in Britain. Witness the "social contract" that was no such thing, or the ceasefire in which terrorism continues, or the lies of politicians on the extent of inflation. This "falsehood explosion" may be the result less of a growth in wickedness than of the way modern communications diffuse the most transparent of political lies.

[6] *The Twilight of Authority*, Heinemann, 1976.

Those who run the bureaucracies include many selfless and dedicated men and women. (It could hardly be otherwise when so large a proportion of the work-force has been turned into state employees.) But they also include politically-motivated groups who seek steadily to elevate the political above the personal (and, indeed, in the highest traditions of *agitprop*, to confuse the two).[7] They arrogate to themselves not only high salaries but also a potential for social engineering that is not based (and cannot be) on any hard social science.

It is not surprising, therefore, that the question arises, as it did, for example, with Professor Antony Flew:[8] "who will equalise the equalisers?" in a progressively collectivist society. Given the problems of parliamentary control, the arrogance and ambitions of some public "servants", and the commitment many of them have (not least within the social services) to their powers as "equalisers", this is a question upon which public concern should be constantly focussed. It is one of the curious legacies of the post-war period that so many of the brightest young people have been sucked into the proliferating "public" services—and have carried over from their education (especially in the social sciences) fantasies of social engineering which coincided neatly with their personal advancement. This was as unfortunate as the syphoning off of talent into the meretricious zones of the press and broadcasting. Both these avenues deprived industry and commerce of considerable talent. A society which ridiculed and enfeebled

[7] A recent, documented critique of this confusion will be found in the posthumously published book by Paul Halmos, *The Personal and the Political,* Hutchinson, 1978.

[8] 'The Procrustean Ideal', in *Encounter*, March 1978, p. 70 *et seq.*

management in the "private sector" and in which the
powers (let alone the self-confidence and rewards) of
management have been degraded in so many places has,
of course, been one in which productivity has fallen
grotesquely.[9] And, of course, the larger the share of the
national income handled by the social engineers the less
flexibility there is for sensible public initiatives and for
the widening of personal choice.

RESISTANCES TO REFORM

What then is to be done? There can be no simple
solution to the political problems that have arisen
through adherence to collectivist social values. The
growth of trade union power, the quietly British "long
march through the institutions" which has proceeded
through the Wilson-Callaghan era, present parallel and
related problems from which the most seasoned politicians fastidiously recoil. The thrust to collective
solidarity rather than reliance on personal effort or
professional standards has infected many strata of
society—well outside the traditional "solidarity" ranks
of organised labour. There is a possibility that inflation,
as it continues—and the escapism among all groups
which inflation has stimulated—will intensify these
trends. Doctors, university teachers and others (seeing
the effects of government policy and of that massive
leveller, inflation) have recourse to, or threaten,
"industrial" action—any inconvenience to the public is,
of course, at once announced as unlikely *and* as deeply
regretted . . .

[9] There is a most interesting discussion of this theme in the
Fawley Foundation Lecture 1977, delivered by the late Professor
John P. Mackintosh, then Labour MP for Berwick & E. Lothian.

Every group learns the rhetoric—the nation of shop-keepers has learned to speak in the accents of trade union leaders. Restraint is acceptable in principle; but in practice every group that can think up a productivity deal seeks to wriggle through the restraints—often proclaiming, simultaneously, an unwavering concern for the sick, the old and the disabled. And since prosperity at home is, in some degree, linked with prosperity abroad as well as with domestic productivity, the economic confusion may well continue.

It could be that the British will accept its continuance —even though it also means a continuing economic decline: and that, as time goes by, they will be content, after much travail, to enjoy a modest standard of life, to reduce their expectations of improvement. They may even be cajoled into letting North Sea oil go to the upkeep of the nationalisers and the social engineers, preferring a limited security to the adventures, let alone the risks, that would come from a change of course. So many now have a vested interest in stagnation, so strong is the instinct against rocking the boat, that this diagnosis might be accurate.

Another outcome could be a tyranny—an authoritarian solution as we sink to the bottom of the industrial societies' league. The man in the street does not aspire to be the man in the gutter—and if tyranny offers an escape from such a fate he might accept the offer. (Intellectuals, of course, should know better: they should reject the snap, siege-economy solutions peddled in so many quarters, solutions that echo, in almost equal proportions, their own naïvety, power-hunger and indifference to freedom.)

A CHANGE OF COURSE

None of this is, however, inevitable. A change of course is, after all, equally conceivable—and it would be premature and perverse to rule it out. There are two prerequisites. One is political will and astuteness at the highest level of government, the other is a shift in social values: and the two, of course, are intimately related.

If the extravagant aims that governments have espoused in economic and social management—and their failures that have spread disillusion—go on, they will bring parliamentary democracy into the deepest contempt. The short-run beneficiaries of bungled policies may purr with contentment: but the broken promises and mendacious justifications, beamed on to every TV screen, could breed powerful anger as well as cynical disillusion. A government which knew its limitations—which widened personal choice while fulfilling its basic duties in the fields of defence, public order and social welfare—would carry much credibility. In these matters effectiveness follows credibility, just as credibility can open reservoirs of loyalty and effectiveness.

I do not believe this is an impossible aim: if I did, I would despair of the democratic process. There must be countless Britons who share this view—who feel that under the slogans of our time we have indeed suffered from "alienated reason". Many, for example, fail to see how there can be *social* justice if, in reality, the State cannot first provide more protection against violence for young people or for old people, or for black and brown people, going about their lawful occasions. Such protection cannot come simply from the police—though the absence or inadequacy of the police is hardly conducive to peace, or justice, in the inner cities. It is also a matter of personal and family discipline.

I do not advocate a return to a mythical "Victorian" ethos, either within the family or the school. The Japanese rate higher than us on these matters—as they do on many economic indices. Could we not learn from them on this *social* achievement without falling victims to "Victorian" repression? These issues, rather than the passions of radical "middle class" intellectuals, are very close to the concerns of ordinary people: and it will not do to dismiss attention to them as an exercise in "populism". There are signs that even educators and churchmen who have stood aloof from these problems —or have simply implied that there is, in any case, a world shortage of virtue as a result of capitalism—are beginning to sniff the wind of change.

Again the irrationalities of "enlightened" housing policies become increasingly clear: the barbarities of recent essays in urban housing, underwritten by experts on taxpayers' money, are now glaringly obvious. They are just as open a target for criticism as the rapacity of property developers or the municipal corruption with which property development has sometimes been aligned. (The homeless, sadly enough, remain homeless: and the new "homes" have become citadels of vandalism and danger.)

CULTURE AND LICENCE

Even within the cultural sphere, the fantasies of the élite egalitarians are subject to bolder scrutiny than was once the case—though observers who attempt such a scrutiny are subject to absurd and malevolent abuse.

Sometimes, in the cultural field, the innovators have overstepped the mark. When, for example, Mr Moss Evans, now life-general-secretary of the Transport and General Workers' Union, sought "a means of policing and enforcing" a code of conduct for the Press many felt his language minatory and disconcerting. "The public", he went on, "are entitled to protection from abuse of the power to influence it. Those who possess these powers must be required to exercise them within the terms of an 'operator's licence'. The qualification for holding such a licence must be the acceptance of clearly defined standards of responsibility and account-ability." Many "ordinary" people—those for whom trade union leaders constantly claim to speak—did not find this declaration exactly reassuring; neither, of course, did many "ordinary" journalists or editors.

THE TIMES ARE A-CHANGING

Even on the economic front, where we are the victims of long-term secular decline as well as bad policies and recently distorted values, there is room for hope. The mysteries of inflation, and its causes, may remain obscure: but the public awareness of its *effects* is better than it was in the early 'seventies. Attention is being redirected to output—and even among the edu-cated classes the contempt for the "private" sector seems to have passed its peak—perhaps in part because openings in the "public" sector have stopped multiply-ing without restraint.

It is possible, therefore, that, in the words of a recently popular radical song, "the times they are a-changing . . .". It would be idle to underrate the resistance of the self-preserving collectivism which has helped to bring us where we are. Those of us who seek to change course —who urge a limited but genuinely caring government, who insist that where our knowledge is so tentative it is foolish and wrong to engage in social engineering— will be denounced as Gradgrinds or as dangerous radicals and populists. Those who seek to preserve, in the Press and the media, a genuine and open focus for debate will be portrayed as lackeys of the Press Lords or enemies of trade unionism. Those who seek to restore self-respect and self-control among the young will be pilloried as heartless and repressive prigs. (There will be many who will hear these things without believing them: but they will remain silent from fear of controversy and, even more, from fear of being on the losing side.)

None of this should deter genuine reformers who seek changes in either the social or cultural spheres. Those who welcome Anthony Burgess's[10] spectre of "TUC-land" will, of course, fight hard to stop us. But we have one strong advantage over our opponents. We recognise the limits of human knowledge and the restraints on human powers. We also know that a dramatic reversal of values will not be achieved overnight. All we may seek, in a living democracy, is that under a limited but friendly government we should be given the chance— and then take the plunge . . .

[10] *1985*, Hutchinson, London, 1978.

Economics and Sociology

CONFRONTATION WITH KEYNES

Ivor Pearce

The Author

IVOR FRANK PEARCE was born in 1916 and educated at Queen Elizabeth's Hospital, Bristol, and at the University of Bristol. He was formerly Lecturer in Economics, University of Nottingham, 1949-56; Reader and Professor of Economics, Institute of Advanced Studies, Australian National University, Canberra, 1956-61; Visiting Fellow, Nuffield College, Oxford, 1961; Professor of Economics and Head of Department, University of Southampton, 1962-72. Since 1973 he has been Director of Research, Econometric Model Building Unit, University of Southampton. He is author of *A Contribution to Demand Analysis* (1964); *International Trade* (1970); *A Model of Output, Employment, Wages and Prices in the UK* (1976); and many other papers in all areas of economics. For the IEA he has contributed an essay, "Stimulants to Exertion . . . A Deficiency of Excitements', in *Catch '76 . . . ?* (Occasional Paper 47, 1976); and a Seminar paper, "Taxing the Dole", in *The State of Taxation* (Readings 16, 1977).

Confrontation with Keynes

"I have a great respect for orthodoxy; not for orthodoxies which prevail in particular schools or nations and which vary from age to age, but for a certain shrewd orthodoxy which the sentiment and practice of laymen maintain everywhere. I think common sense, in a rough dogged way, is technically sounder than special schools of philosophy, each of which squints and overlooks half the facts and half the difficulties in its eagerness to find in some detail the key to the whole."

GEORGE SANTAYANA   (*Scepticism and Animal Faith*)

*   *   *

The course of human history is guided not by new ideas, for there are none, but by contemporary conventional wisdom, that is, by some ephemeral sub-group of the totality of old ideas, often believed to be new, seized upon as the currently agreed solution to whatever difficulties immediate experience has made to seem important, and congealed into a crust of dogma by endless repetition and obeisance.

Providentially the impermanence of conventional wisdom is ensured by its own capacity for self-annihilation. It carries within itself the seeds of its own destruction. It cannot but prove itself to be false, incomplete, or something of both. Pressed to its logical conclusion it calls for action quite obviously inconsistent with the commonest of common sense.

THE "RIGHT" NOT TO BE POOR

Consider simply the problem of poverty. This might be supposed, at least in principle, to be the most easily managed of all social evils; for all that is necessary is to institute "fair shares". Where poverty is extreme it is easy to gain near-universal approval for a measure of income redistribution. It is natural to imagine, and indeed to hope for, a world entirely free of poverty. The point might even be reached where, according to prevailing conventional wisdom, the slightest hint that there could be advantage to society if some degree of poverty were permitted in some circumstances would call for immediate condemnation if not penalty. But no such orthodoxy could survive for long. Powerfully held beliefs inevitably generate action, which just as inevitably reveal the need for second thoughts. Each successive step towards the supposed Utopia draws attention ever more insistently to inconvenient facts of life, always known but only too easily overlooked.

In the first place, it could not long escape notice that, in the absence of perfect equality of both income and wealth, at least one person could, with justice, claim to be poor. Experiment would verify the simple truth that to grant to everyone the "right" not to be poor is to deny to everyone the right to be rich. To seek actively to improve the welfare of self or family is *ipso facto* to seek actively to condemn everyone else to poverty.

Conceivably of course it might at first be agreed that it is more important that no-one should be poor than it is that someone should be rich. The rights of those who prefer wealth to leisure could be over-ridden and their freedom to work for gain suppressed. But even then the notion of a basic human right not to be poor could not survive its attainment; for to abolish poverty is to abolish the need to labour which is, outside of the Garden of Eden, to abolish wealth itself.

Simplistic ideas put into practice—and almost all "ideas" are simplistic—necessarily founder in the ocean of common sense upon which from time to time they surface. Characteristically, we observe throughout history cycles of conventional wisdom alternating between over-reverence for equality and over-emphasis of the importance of self-help depending on the extent to which recent experience has attracted public attention to the folly of its opposite. But this is not a matter for despair. Rather it is a cause for wonder at the magic of a providential arrangement which, despite the best efforts of unthinking idealists to change it, continues to preserve for ever both the opportunity to exercise the virtue of charity and the stimulus to avoid the sin of sloth.

FASHIONABLE BELIEFS WILL NOT LAST

Happily also the impermanence of conventional wisdom furnishes another, perhaps less metaphysical, occasion for satisfaction. In looking into the future as far as 1989 we may be sure of at least one thing. A fair proportion of today's fashionable beliefs will not be fashionable eleven years hence. Nor is it difficult to identify some of those beliefs and to predict changes which must follow their toppling. In particular, the time has come to reconsider the group of arguments known collectively to conventional wisdom as "The Keynesian Revolution".

"The Keynesian Revolution" was a revolution not in economic thought but a turnabout in another sense of the cycle of conventional wisdom and of government behaviour. It introduced no new fundamental idea and in detail it is mostly incorrect or incomplete. Its theoretical underpinning consists of little more than an unnecessarily technical version of the age-old under-consumptionist claim that the economic system can be, and frequently is, chronically threatened by a general failure of effective demand for goods produced. Today, although with growing uncertainty, "conventional wisdom" continues to assert the following propositions all of which have, in recent years, dramatically demonstrated their falsity in practice.

The somewhat closely reasoned argument that follows, marked by asterisks, could be skipped by readers more interested in what is false than in why it must be false.

*   *   *

DEMAND CREATES SUPPLY, OR
SALVATION BY EMPTY-BOTTLE-BURYING

The principal article of faith pervading all modern macro-economic theory teaches that production *follows*, and is inevitably induced by, spending. If and only if consumers spend more, it is claimed, will producers produce more.

In the real world the truth is exactly the reverse. Only if producers produce more can real incomes and hence real spending rise. No special expertise is necessary to understand this principle. It is simply and obviously a matter of fact. Wages are ordinarily paid *before* goods produced are sold, not after. It is for this reason, and no other, that industry must have money capital *before* it can increase production. The entrepreneur raises capital to pay wages which he recovers on the sale of the product, thereby acquiring funds to pay wages again in the next round. The larger is production, the higher the wages paid and hence the more the demand for the product. How could anyone believe anything different? Yet under the influence of modern under-consumptionism we do!—or did.

Under-consumptionists today put the argument in reverse. If there is unemployment, it is thought, money should be delivered into the hands of consumers who will then induce production, and hence employment, by spending. Sadly this attractive doctrine also is false.

In *The General Theory of Employment, Interest and Money* J. M. Keynes wrote that if no other work can be found printed money might be buried in glass bottles to be disinterred by the otherwise unemployed who, for their pains, would be allowed to keep and spend any notes they recovered. The resulting extra spending would then encourage production and still more employment. But how could the money ever be spent? Digging up bottles produces no goods to buy, except perhaps empty bottles. There must be too much money chasing too few goods. Inflation will occur, or there will be an excess of imports over exports, goods to buy having been brought in from overseas. It is obvious that, if the unemployed are to be offered work, that very work must be designed to bring into being the food and clothing which the newly employed will want to buy with the incomes they have earned. Nothing else makes sense.

It is possible, of course, to believe that the sight of

large numbers of people possessed of money they are unable to spend would tempt businessmen to *try* to produce more goods. But where would the money needed to pay the increase in the wage bill now come from? Cash flow derives from hard sales, not from unrealised expectations. Nor is this all. Even if producers did find the money to increase output, any realised increase must generate still more income (spending power) equal in value to the goods produced. In no way is it possible to manufacture more goods without at the same time generating incomes sufficient to buy them. In no way therefore could the printed money buried in Keynes's bottles ever be absorbed into the system without causing either a rise in prices or an excess of imports over exports. Who can doubt this is what we have observed in recent years?

Today's conventional wisdom teaches us to disregard two simple common-sense rules which have long been understood by more thoughtful economists. These rules require, first, that, if there are unemployed resources such as labour, purchasing power should be put into the hands of those who are going to buy *labour* and not into the hands of those who would try to buy *consumer goods*. That is, newly created credit, if it is called for, should be made available only to *producers,* not to consumers. The second rule says that money should be made available only to producers *who have idle capital resources and work-in-progress*, capable of bringing into being at once, precisely that flow of consumer goods which the newly employed will wish to buy.

Despite Keynes's belief to the contrary, the creation of capital, sometimes a necessary precondition for increased employment, demands an act of saving. If money is printed to be spent on capital goods, incomes will be generated, once again with no corresponding consumer goods to buy. Inflation is unavoidable. Indeed the inflation which must follow is no more than nature's device for "forcing" upon the community the real saving without which an increase in the capital stock is impossible. Keynes argued vociferously that the required saving could come from the production of the formerly unemployed. But of course it cannot. It is true that a once-and-for-all act of saving makes a higher amount of employment possible *for ever*; and from it more saving might be expected. But the secondary saving will not occur at all without the primary saving which makes it possible.

Reckless disregard of this common sense is the cause of the present world-wide inflation. Negotiated wage increases, frequently blamed, constitute one of the many possible ways of ignoring that common sense. Before very long inflation itself will destroy the conventional wisdom which allows inflation to flourish.

SALVATION THROUGH PUBLIC WORKS

The natural extension of the bottle-burying prescription is the perennial demand, dating at least from around 2,000 BC, for government spending on public works. If there are unemployed, the argument goes, how absurd it is not to set them to work building valuable roads and hospitals. If there is no money, it should be printed.

Gentle reader, you will hardly now need to be prompted. Roads and hospitals are not ordinarily offered for sale. The printed monies used to buy the services of the construction industry become incomes, but, as before, there are no consumer goods to buy with them. Inflation must therefore follow. Hospitals and roads are desirable utilities, but there is no escaping paying for them.

Public works, if they are not to cause inflation, must be financed out of taxation or by the genuine borrowing of part of the current income of persons. "Borrowing" from bank-created credit is not admissible since this is equivalent to the printing of money.[1]

Is this not all common sense? Why should we suppose that the enterprise of government directed towards the production of public works might be able to achieve more in the way of employment than the enterprise of government, or anyone else, directed towards the production of anything else? Are we so obsessed by the desire to create demand by public works that we fail to note that the only thing we can stimulate without inflation is the production of goods we intend to buy?

If we want more hospitals more urgently than more bread, then hospitals should be built. But it makes no sense to produce hospitals because involuntary unemployment exists when what we really want is bread. The unemployed should then bake bread, not build hospitals. And why should it be thought to be more appropriate

[1] At the point of introduction of the policy some degree of finesse is necessary in the timing. Money should be printed to pay the unemployed for *one time-period only*. At the same time, taxes on borrowing from the public must be introduced to finance all further payments to those engaged on public works. The expenditure of the formerly unemployed will then match the reduction in consumer expenditure due to taxation leaving the total production and sales of consumer goods unchanged. Overall gross production per time-period will have risen without inflation by the value of the new public works, that is, by the amount of new money printed strictly in accord with the age-old quantity theory of money rejected by Keynes.

for government to organise production? Might it not be more sensible to inquire into the *impediments* to production facing the rest of the community and remove *them*?

The emphasis on government participation finds its origin in the myth that what is lacking is demand rather than supply. This notion is false. The belief that the community can somehow "spend its way out of unemployment"[2] is so obviously wrong that it would at once be rejected by everyone were it not that conventional wisdom conditions people who come to the arguments for the first time to accept that what they are about to be told is true *even before they consider the logic*. A sufficient weight of public opinion can convince almost anyone of almost anything, as the next section will show.

THE MYTH OF THE MULTIPLIER

It is commonly said that an increase in government spending will raise employment by an amount many times larger in value than the original sum of money injected. A "multiplier effect" is supposed to operate as follows.

Money spent by government raises the demand for, and hence the production of, commodities. But more production creates more incomes which are again spent on commodities, still further raising production and incomes and so on. Except that "leakages" occur due to the *saving* (not spending) of some fraction of the incomes generated in each round, additional govern-

[2] Mr James Callaghan saw through this "myth" in September 1976.

ment spending of one pound would lead at once to full employment.

This is an argument of breathtaking lunacy, wrong on all conceivable counts. Yet it continues to be pressed in its crudest form by even the most respectable of authorities.[3] To see why it must be wrong, suppose there were no savings and hence no "leakages". Suppose further that excess demand always and at once induces a corresponding increase in production, contrary to everything that has been said above. Even then it would still not be true that a single injection of government spending could do more than raise the gross national product (GNP) *per period of time* by precisely the sum of money injected. One pound properly spent might raise production by one pound. The one pound of income generated, however, would be needed to buy the one pound's worth of extra production. The money passes back to the producer who uses it to pay the wages required to sustain the extra one pound of production in the next period of time. Those wages again buy the production in period two. Employment and output will have risen by only *one* pound's worth. *There is no multiplier.* The value of GNP over the time it takes for money to circulate once is equal to the quantity of money, a proposition observed and noted by economists again and again over hundreds of years; they called it "the quantity theory of money".

If the government were to inject new money over and over again in every period there would be an increase in the *value* (not usually the *quantity*) of the GNP in every period until at last, after an infinite time, prices

[3] For example, *The Economist,* 21 January, 1978, p. 94: "Double Your Money".

and the value of the gross national product would reach
infinity. But again the Egyptians of 2,000 BC knew this,
as did, and does, every economist who has ever lived
since. An infinite supply of money implies infinite
prices.

THE KEYNESIAN MULTIPLIER

Naturally Keynes did not claim the existence of a
multiplier in this sense. By the use of the term multiplier, however, he did revive the myth,[4] at the same
time encouraging a text-book theory which is hardly
less absurd. Keynes's argument is best explained as
follows.

If consumers spend, say, nine-tenths of their income
and save the balance, and if supply is to equal demand,
then nine-tenths of all goods produced must be consumer goods and services and one-tenth must be capital
goods financed by saving. Incomes generated and spent
equal the total value of goods produced as explained
above. It follows that as long as the propensity to
consume remains in the ratio 9:1 there must be nine
times as many consumer goods produced as capital
goods. One whole chapter of Keynes's *General Theory*
is given to an account of the reasons why we should
expect the "propensity to consume" to remain constant
come what may. The rest is easy.

If the production of consumer goods must always be
nine times the production of investment goods it has to
be true that any policy which can raise the production

[4] John Law (1671-1729) successfully used the argument, thereby
achieving notoriety as the principal architect of the Mississippi
Bubble. The same "idea" recurs with sufficient frequency to
suggest that Law was not the first to think of it.

of investment goods by, say, one pound's worth must *ipso facto* raise *total* production by 10 times that amount. The multiplier is 10.

The logic of this theory is indisputable, but its premises are quixotic. They recall the race-horse owner who was fond of explaining that the secret of winning races is to get the tail of the animal first past the post: the rest of it was sure to be there too.

Keynes's followers[5] later compounded the felony by developing a scenario, rather like the multiplier, purporting to show how the tail might after all be the prime mover. But again, like the multiplier story itself, this contradicts common sense in almost every respect.

If money is printed to stimulate investment in capital goods, extra income will be generated. But, because only capital goods have at this point been produced, with no consumer goods in proportion, there must be an excess demand for consumer goods and a deficit demand for the investment goods already in existence. The excess demand for consumer goods will, it is supposed, stimulate the production of consumer goods, so that more money can be printed to buy the capital goods over-produced. The new cash injection will sustain the production of capital goods, so creating still more excess demand for consumer goods, and hence still more production. Successive injections of cash *via* investment, as required by the quantity theory of money, will after an infinite time raise the production of consumer goods to nine times that of the once-for-all increase in the *rate* of investment per time-period, thus restoring at last the supply-equals-demand condition postulated by Keynes.

[5] Any textbook entitled *An Introduction to Macro-Economics* or its equivalent.

No more perfect subject for ridicule could be imagined than this strange prescription for economic recovery. Even if it were true (which it is not for reasons given above) that consumer spending in excess of supply always and immediately induces an increase in production without inflation, the whole idea remains especially odd. If it really is possible, by printing money or by other means, to encourage the production of capital goods, for what extraordinary reason do we not do the same with consumer goods in the proportions in which both kinds of goods are going to be bought? This way supply and demand will be equal at all times, and the desired rise in production would be brought about at once. Why put money into the system in the wrong place in penny packets when it can easily be introduced in the right place all at once?

Common sense, efficiency and the pursuit of profit combine to recommend that we should try to produce what we want to buy. Conventional wisdom, on the other hand, advises that we produce what the public does *not* want and will *not* buy, partly to generate *excess* demand for the goods it does want and partly to impose a lame-duck status on the capital goods industry, affording thereby an excuse to continue to print money for the production of *unwanted* goods in every time-period, just to sustain indefinitely the excess demand for consumer goods, mistakenly supposed to be the *sine qua non* of increased production.

The world has become so obsessed with the "idea" that only demand can induce supply that it supports proposals to generate excess demand for some goods by supplying too much of others. Believing passionately that only demand can stimulate supply, it relies, with infinite irony, upon *supply* to create the demand it is so anxious about. What could be the origin of such a strange idea?

SAVING AND HOARDING

The periodic successes throughout history of under-consumptionism rest largely upon the fact that the doctrine preaches always what we want to hear. Chapter 24 of Keynes's *General Theory of Employment, Interest and Money* promises everything including (yes, it really is there) more than a hint that, because the most serious economic problems had (in the preceding pages) been solved, we might now expect to see the end not only of poverty but even of war between nations! Alas, it cannot be so.

Without labour there can be no consumption, without the redeployment of labour there can be no change, without saving there can be no capital. Labour is unpleasant, redeployment is unpleasant, saving requires sacrifice of consumption. Economic pressures signal the need to engage in these unpleasant activities. A shortage of money, in normal times, simply indicates that the person experiencing the shortage is not performing as a producer those duties he is demanding of himself as a consumer. Common sense cries out that the printing of money can be no solution. But common sense warns us also to expect that in unguarded moments we will be tempted to suppose that it is.

For these reasons it is not at all surprising that again and again throughout the ages attempts have been made to refute Say's Law which holds that only supply can create satisfiable demand. This law is a question of *fact*, not a matter of logic. It need not be true. Nobody has ever disputed the truism that production generates incomes. What is disputed is whether or not the income generated is always spent. It is easy to imagine the existence of an army of misers hoarding currency in secret places, taking pleasure in counting it daily. Under-consumptionists in the past have always made much of this vision. Demand could fail because consumers hoard. If we could believe in hoarding we could believe in the need to print and distribute money to consumers to replace the currency lost into hoards. *This is the origin of the doctrine that demand is necessary for supply.* If producers cannot sell what they produce, they will reduce their demand for labour.

Consider the attractions of this doctrine. Producers who have failed to redeploy labour in response to change and employees who are unwilling to allow themselves to be redeployed will see in it both an excuse for their failure and a means to escape the consequences. Print money to buy the things that nobody wants. This way labour can go on producing the things that nobody wants. The whole can be blamed by everyone on the hoarders of money instead of their own unwillingness to be bothered to produce things that people do want. At the same time there is unlikely to be any objection from consumers to proposals to give them printed money and encourage them to spend it. One consumer, the government, takes particular pleasure in spending in excess of income. Reduced taxation, apparently without reduction of benefits, is always good for votes.

Unfortunately, or perhaps fortunately, there has never really been any significant hoarding in any age. To hoard is totally irrational. Money today may be deposited in a bank where, not only is it safer than it would be under the bed, it earns interest and may be withdrawn at a moment's notice. Nor has it ever been different. Two thousand years ago, in the parable, the servant who buried his master's talent of silver was admonished "thou oughtest at least to have put my money with the exchangers then at my coming I should have received mine own with usury". Exchangers spend, they do not hoard.

It should be understood at once that *saving* is not *hoarding*. Saving is a demand for earning assets or, alternatively, a demand for borrowers who borrow to spend more than they earn, paying interest for the privilege. In the UK at the present time the government stands ready to borrow and spend anything that anyone may choose to save.

Keynes argued, first, that there is no hoarding and, second, that there is. He emphasised first that, if what is saved is not spent, demand will fail. Production, incomes and hence saving will then fall until the hoarding is eliminated. There will be no observable hoarding because, if it appears, it will, in the twinkling of an eye, be eliminated by changes in the level of employment. According to Keynes, therefore, hoarding is like the philosopher's black cat which sits in a dark cupboard. It cannot be seen because it disappears as soon as one opens the cupboard door to look for it. What is not explained is where the money disappears to. Money is money. Somebody has it. Perhaps the explanation lies in Keynes's alternative idea?

In the *General Theory* strong emphasis is placed on "liquidity preference". This is hoarding which supposedly takes the form of "idle" bank balances. The search for these idle balances has for some years now provided both profit and entertainment for an ever-increasing corps of economists who report their findings in papers under the generic title "Estimating the Demand for Money". But the truth is that bank balances are never left idle. Money not lent at interest is held for spending, not for saving. Money can of course be annihilated by the repayment of bank advances, but only if the bank can find no alternative borrower, an unlikely circumstance at the present time. Furthermore, bank advances are made primarily to producers, not to consumers. They are repaid, when they are repaid, by producers who have decided not to produce, not by consumers who have decided not to consume.[6]

The myth of the hoarder remains a myth. The consequences of the myth have been catastrophic. The myth will be exploded by events which are a consequence of the myth.

* * *

THE END OF THE AFFAIR

By 1989 the great inflation of the 1970s will be over. The ideas which supported it will have come again to be recognised as the naïve beliefs which succeed for a while because of their superficial attractiveness only to fail in the end, destroyed by the very effects of their acceptance. The recreation of a new-old conventional wisdom, perhaps little better than that which preceded it, is a process which cannot be hurried. Events and good sense will in due course erase the excesses of those who "in their eagerness to find in some detail the key

[6] Those who doubt should study Tables 13.2 to 13.10 in the Blue Book, *National Income and Expenditure*.

to the whole"[7] came for a while to believe in solutions to *economic problems which by their very nature have no solution.*

The academic exegesis within asterisks above can play no part in the process of erasure for it is no more than a particle of the process itself. It is but a faint echo of an eternal truth which history is once again teaching us.

Arguments do not convince. They merely give comfort to those who, seized by an "idea", determine to put it into practice. The "idea" once rooted can be destroyed only by the absurdities made evident by its practice.

Already throughout the world the absurdities of under-consumptionism are more than apparent. All that is necessary is to look around. The price mechanism, without which no economic system can survive, is everywhere seriously undermined. We have a situation which would have been predicted at once by any competent economist of the late 19th century, supposing that any of them could have been persuaded that the 20th century would behave so foolishly. Policies have been implemented formerly associated only with the behaviour of the most irresponsible of governments. Exactly as in the past, public forgery, with the attitude of mind that goes with it, has been accompanied by a multiplication of banking and international banking activities both damaging and unnecessary. Money printing exercises now extend to the semi-official forging not only of the national currency but of that of every other country as well. (The total of US$ deposits in

[7] George Santayana—the full quotation is on p. 93.

Euro-dollar accounts currently exceeds $500 billions, that is, about one and one-half times all of the money in the United States itself. Only a very small proportion of this money could have originated in the USA.)

On a scale never before known, money has failed in its essential role as a store of value. Trading is everywhere more profitable than production. Losses are called "capital gains" and are taxed. Real gains of people in debt are called costs and are subsidised. Wages and prices are no longer accepted as facts of life determined by the value to society of the goods or services to which they are attached; rather they have become matters for "negotiation", an exercise in which both political power and power of a cruder kind have proved themselves more effective than proof of increased worth. The less scrupulous make use of accounting conventions belonging to other times to defraud those bound by law and common practice to accept contracts which in real terms are obviously "weighted". There is more gain in "demanding" a larger share of the national product than in adding to it. The decline in commercial, and hence social, morality always associated with inflation is universal. Prudence and thrift are penalised. Negligence and improvidence are indemnified with no premium demanded.

Adam Smith did not doubt that employment and the wealth of nations are simultaneously begotten by the energy and initiative of those who organise production, not by consumers who enjoy the fruits. Could any proposition be more obvious? Yet it is the consumer who is coddled and enterprise which is harassed.

Trade union leaders sometimes call for action to reduce unemployment, yet all the time the opportunity to reduce unemployment lies in their own hands. Trade unions have money and are well placed to raise more. Why do they not found industries of their own thereby earning, simultaneously, a profit, the gratitude of consumers, and the thanks of the members they are pledged to serve?

It does not matter who organises production. What matters is that it should be organised. It does not matter who owns capital. What matters is that somebody should. If the ownership of capital confers no reward, no-one will accumulate capital and no-one will take care that what we have is not frittered away. In the same way, those who organise production must be rewarded in proportion to their success. If they are not, they will not try to succeed. They will try only to be rewarded.

Could it be that the Keynesian Revolution has encouraged us to forget these simple truths? If so, nothing could be more conducive to economic decline.

POLITICO-MEGALOMANIA: UTOPIA THROUGH REGULATION

Above all, the Keynesian Revolution seems to have fertilised a bumper harvest of politico-megalomania. It is a short step from the belief that unemployment can be controlled by "policy" to the belief that the government can deal with any economic ill whatever, and, what is worse, to the belief that it *ought* to do so. It is right that the working of the economic system should be carefully studied. It is right to use all knowledge available to procure a stable environment within which individuals might be free to pursue their economic interests with confidence that the institutional arrangements upon which they rely will not suddenly collapse. It may even be right that, with more study, we shall one day learn how this is to be done.

What is not right is to imagine that it will ever be possible to dispense with prices and wages and to achieve Utopia through detailed government regulation. This is not because detailed regulation is necessarily impossible, although at present, the modern computer notwithstanding, it is well beyond the capacity of any system we know how to implement. Rather it is because any system other than the price system is an affront to human dignity. The only alternative to the price mechanism is a command society where individual choice is replaced by government decree. Nor is this all. The absence of, or arbitrary nature of, prices in a command society conceals from the community all knowledge of the physical constraints against which the struggle for survival is conducted. Not only is the individual denied the right to choose; he is denied even the right to know the set of alternatives from which the government chooses for him.

What can never be right also is that it should continue to be thought reasonable and proper to support a system in which more than 70 per cent of the gross national income earned by individuals is channelled first into the hands of committees which disburse the whole in fringe benefits to whomever they see fit. *A fortiori* it cannot be right that any part of the funds so channelled should be redirected from one committee to another and hence to yet another with unknown amounts lost in the interstices. One hundred years ago fringe benefits were called "truck" and the "truck system" slavery. We should be grateful to HRH Prince

Philip for his timely reminder elsewhere in this volume that a society which lives upon fringe benefits is a society of slaves (p. 218).

Happily there are signs that the madness is ending. It is coming slowly but surely to be understood that, as long as new rules and regulations continue to pour out from the legislature at the present rate, they cannot possibly all be read, much less understood—even by lawyers. Frequently their ambiguity is such that their meaning remains unknown even to those charged with the duty of administering them. Experience has taught most of us to expect that each new policy announcement will be followed, like the one which preceded it, by its evident failure and a course of events totally unpredicted and sometimes hardly imagined. There are comforting signs that policy-makers are beginning to lose, at last, the Keynesian confidence which formerly encouraged them in the face of each current disaster to echo the thoughts of Alice, once again in the long low hall: "next time we shall do better". The belief that the government conductor of the economic orchestra knows the score is wearing more than a little thin. Perhaps by 1989 he will have been persuaded to step down and to allow the instrumentalists to have another go on their own. Many little mistakes are not likely to be heard. But a single error by the conductor brings the music to a halt.

Perhaps we can hope that in one way or another proper economic discipline will in the not too distant future be restored and the failure of the "great" experiment will be acknowledged. Whatever is due to happen, one truth must certainly be faced anew. We have at least to learn again that economic pressures are not simply unnecessary evils against which protection can be provided by government. They reflect a reality against which protection is impossible.

Economics and Sociology

CAN WE ESCAPE?

Max Hartwell

The Author

RONALD MAX HARTWELL was born in 1921 and edu-
cated at the Universities of New England and Sydney
(Australia) and Oxford. Since 1978 he has been Joint-
Director of the Centre for Socio-Legal Studies, Wolfson
College, Oxford and Faculty Fellow, Nuffield College,
Oxford. He was formerly Reader in Recent Social and
Economic History, University of Oxford, 1956-77.

Before Oxford he was Professor of Economic History
and Dean of the Faculty of Humanities and Social
Sciences, University of New South Wales. He has been
a Visiting Professor in the University of Ibadan,
Nigeria, the Australian National University, Canberra,
and the University of Virginia, Charlottesville.

Editor of *The Economic History Review,* 1957-72.
Dr Hartwell's publications include: *The Economic
Development of Van Diemens Land, 1820-1850* (1954);
(ed.) *The Causes of the Industrial Revolution* (1967);
(ed.) *The Industrial Revolution* (1970); *The Industrial
Revolution and Economic Growth* (1971); (with R. W.
Breach) *British Economy and Society, 1870-1970* (1972);
and articles in learned journals. For the IEA he con-
tributed an essay, "The Consequences of the Industrial
Revolution in England for the Poor", in *The Long
Debate on Poverty* (Readings 9, 1972; 2nd Edition,
1974).

Can We Escape?

I

DECLINE OF THE INDIVIDUAL:
THE "PUBLIC TRAP"

"Liberty and responsibility are inseparable", Hayek has written.

> "Liberty not only means that the individual has both the opportunity and the burden of choice; it also means that he must bear the consequences of his actions and will receive praise or blame for them."[1]

In Britain the responsibilities of government are continually expanding while those of the individual are continually contracting. There has been, in consequence, a retreat from freedom; as the individual's responsibilities are taken from him, so his ability and willingness to accept responsibility decline, and government has to take over more responsibilities. As government grows more active, the individual grows more passive, and intervention becomes an imperative. The process is a vicious circle, *a responsibility trap* or *a public[2] trap*, which has led to the almost universal acceptance of a

[1] F. A. Hayek, *The Constitution of Liberty*, University of Chicago Press, 1960, p. 71.

[2] "Public" here means "state" or "government", an old usage preferred by advocates of government intervention because it sounds more acceptable.

119

substantial and increasing role for the state in all of our affairs. Indeed, at a certain point the retreat from freedom becomes a fear of freedom, an avoidance of responsibility, a feeling of helplessness in the face of needs and problems, a willing dependency on, and a fearful servility towards, government and its agencies.

What has caused the retreat from freedom? Why has the range and quantity of goods and services provided by the state increased constantly in the 20th century? Why should the state now have the role of almost universal provider? Why should the state also have the role of almost universal solver of social problems? Why, indeed, have most problems become *public* problems? And, perhaps most puzzling of all, why is there widespread belief that the state can provide goods and services efficiently, and solve social problems effectively? After all, although government provides some goods— education, for example—it does not provide others— like holidays. Although government is preoccupied with some social problems—inequalities of wealth and income, for example—it neglects others—incitement to class hatred, for example. And although government produces many goods and services, it usually produces them less efficiently than the private sector[3] and, moreover, is demonstrably unable to achieve declared objectives in most of its endeavours.

THE "PUBLIC" TRAP
The answers to these questions and paradoxes lie in the history of a mutually reinforcing web of incremental in-

---

[3] "The private sector" of an economy, as opposed to "the public sector", is that part of the economy which is in private hands, privately owned and privately managed.

creases in government that constituted, and still constitutes, a trap, *the public trap*. A trap, says the Concise Oxford Dictionary, is a "pitfall or enclosure . . . for catching animals, affording entrance but not exit and often baited". Most increases in government have been achieved by offering inducements,[4] almost invariably economic, and most of such increases have been difficult, if not impossible, to reverse; hence, they are aptly described as traps.

The combined effect of such traps has been to produce "the *they* complex", the prevailing attitude of mind which, faced with a problem, expresses itself in the effortless phrase, " 'They' should do something about it", and not in the purposeful phrase, " 'I' will do something about it". The replacement of "they", meaning government, for "I", meaning the individual, reflects a remarkable decline since the 19th century in a robust sense of personal responsibility.

Responsibilities are now for governments; individuals have rights rather than responsibilities. And rights are carefully defined and circumscribed, usually by government rather than by some moral consensus. Notably, governments have assumed the responsibility of controlling social processes, of making the important decisions about society and economy, leaving the individual to make an ever-narrowing range of increasingly unimportant decisions.

Paradoxically, as wealth has increased, as individuals have improved their material well-being, and, on

---

[4] The National Enterprise Board is a good example, a government agency offering inducements both to "the left" and "the right"—to socialists who want state ownership and to industrialists who want financial support.

common-sense reasoning, their ability to look after themselves, governments have acted as though that ability has declined. If much of the growth of government was a response to the poverty of a proportion of the population, government should have declined as poverty declined. Instead government's response to an increasingly wealthy society has been to expand the welfare state, not to reduce it, as though government is an "income-elastic" consumer good, the demand for which increases with rising income.

FROM SELF-HELP TO HAND-OUT

The result has been the replacement of the ethic of self-help by the ethic of hand-out, the ethic of the reservation, that ethic of the way of life imposed by the state on the unfortunate American Indians or Australian aborigines, in which values of self-respect, self-reliance and work are eroded by making the individual almost entirely a pensioner, dependent on the state for most of his essential requirements. And as the range of life choices and the willingness to accept responsibility decline, so too the willingness to accept the consequences of individual actions declines.

The denial of responsibility for individual actions is perhaps the most damaging moral consequence of the growth of government; it makes it difficult to blame anybody for anything; it produces, in the long run, a no-fault society in which all damages are paid for by government. Two beliefs, formulated by the intellectuals, exculpate the individual from feelings of blame for the things he does: first, the conviction, developed and sustained by historians, that the individual is controlled by exogenous social forces over which he has no control; second, the conviction, developed by the social scientists, that the individual is the involuntary victim of internally generated psychological forces which he does not understand and cannot control. Thus the *responsibilities* of the individual have declined, along with the *sense of responsibility* for the consequences of the actions he does take. This two-fold decline has weakened motivation and energy. The result has been a trivialising of life, a decline in charity and concern for others, a decline in tolerance and acceptance of in-dividual differences, a decline in morality, and, above all, a decline in freedom. These are the consequences of *the public trap* into which the British have fallen.

II

WHITTLING AWAY OF THE STATE

Why have we fallen into the public trap? Can we escape?

Unfortunately, from the point of view of a strategy of escape, there is no easy solution. There is no great es-cape possible. The large and growing public trap is a combination of traps, of differing histories and con-sequences, and with differing solutions. If we are to restore responsibilities and a sense of responsibility to the individual, escape from the trap must take the form of a complex of withdrawing operations. As the growth of government has been continuous over a long period, and not one great fall of man, so escape will be, if pos-sible, a similar process, a whittling away of the power of the state rather than a revolution of decline. The process, institutionally, will be something like Fabianism in reverse; the results will resemble the Marxist false dream of the withering away of the state under socialism, but the withering will be the result of positive actions of reducing state power, not an involuntary decline. The process will take the form both of changing views, and of changing institutions, with the determined aims of escape from the network of government, and of restoration of individual freedoms. To be effective the campaign against government will ensure that there is widespread recognition of the reality of the public trap, and that there are, also, means of escape. Even a simplified analysis reveals the magnitude of the problem and some of the solutions.

On the side of ideas, there have been two main traps:

the social science trap, an unfortunate consequence of the development of the social sciences, with their tendency to analyse society in the aggregate, to see all problems as social rather than as individual, and to believe in social engineering, in the possibility of manipulating society to conform to some design or plan;

the élitist trap or *the activist intellectual trap,* an unfortunate consequence of the growth of the intelligentsia, of professional and technical specialists of high ability and advanced education who, like a new aristocracy, see themselves as the natural leaders of the new and complex society of industrialisation, and who not only know what people want (or should want), but are active in seeing they get what they want (or rather what the élite knows they want).

On the side of institutions, there have been three main traps:

the incremental government growth trap, the character of government to advance by approved increments, so that while any particular increment constitutes a small increase in government, the total of such increments over time constitutes a massive increase;

the public inquiry trap, the propensity that has developed since the industrial revolution to investigate identified social problems by public inquiry, with the almost inevitable consequence of solving them by public action;

the bureaucratic trap, the seemingly inevitable tendency of bureaucracies of control, once established, to enlarge their responsibilities, power and influence, and personnel, and thus to grow and never to decline.

III

THE IDEAS TRAPS

The social science trap is the frame of mind, the approach to society and economy, the bias in social policy, which predisposes acceptance of the essentially public character of all social phenomena, and which sustains the belief that society is a complex organisation that can be managed and manipulated. Before the development of the social sciences, the accepted study of man was history, both ancient and modern; and history, from which practical lessons could be learned, was concerned with individuals, their motivations and actions. History, because it was past experience, was the proper study for men of affairs, especially politicians. The social sciences, however, promised much more: they dealt with (indeed invented most) social aggregates; they claimed quantitative accuracy, analytical sophistication, and predictive ability; more than that— they also raised the possibility of the social manipulation of large groups. History had been neither analytical nor prescriptive; its lessons had been warnings rather than prescriptions; it had no laws and allowed for the contingent and unpredictable. The social sciences were quantitative, analytical and prescriptive; they made possible (or seemed to make possible) the art of social engineering or social architecture, of moulding society to design or plan, of solving social problems by government decision.

Increasingly, from the mid-19th century onwards, age-old social problems that had been attributed largely to the individual, and whose solutions had been seen largely as the responsibility of individuals (either directly or through charity—the activity of other individuals), were now analysed in terms of social determinants beyond the control of the individual. All problems were becoming social or public, and public problems needed public solutions.

The tendency was accelerated by the systematic collection of social data; indeed, until social trends could be measured, the magnitude of social problems could not be comprehended, nor could remedial public action be planned and budgeted for. Increasingly, also, the social scientists argued for social engineering, a practical art that appealed strongly to ambitious and well-intentioned politicians. Given desirable ends, the social scientists said, it was possible to direct society towards those ends; society was a sort of large machine or building whose mechanism or shape could be changed by conscious planning and bureaucratic manipulation. This was the most acceptable but the most dangerous legacy that the social sciences bequeathed to 20th-century government. Thus, all social problems were now not only public; they could also be solved by government intervention.

The activist intellectual trap is the result of the desire and ambition of the majority of intellectuals not only to understand society but to change it, not only to be positive or neutral in their analysis of society but to be normative, not only to be the objective spectators of social change but to be actors in history, and with important roles. The activist intellectual combines specialist and technical expertise, which gives him authority, and utopianism, which gives him moral purpose. The combination is a recipe for action, indeed leadership, in practical affairs. It is a feature of 20th-century society that intellectuals are the most active group giving social advice and that their role has been increasingly participatory in the administration of social policy.

Intellectuals since the Enlightenment have been concerned with social reform, and since their position in society has enabled them to influence ideas and policy, and since their inclinations have been activist, they have been agents for the expansion of government. Intellectuals write books (influencing the general reading public), teach (influencing the student population, the next generation of business men and politicians), and often help to administer the policies they recommend. Lacking usually the wealth and status of the aristocracy and of the business and professional classes, the intellectuals have created a status for themselves, that of planners and monitors of social reform. They identify social problems and recommend solutions; they establish themselves as specialists in social problems and as progressive reformers. In particular they assume in an élite fashion that they are both the standard-setters, who determine what the world should be like, and also the appropriate social engineers, who know how to achieve the desired world. They are, usually, more interested in making people do particular things than in allowing them to do what they like; they are more concerned with moulding people to desired ends than in ensuring their individuality, responsibility and freedoms.

IV

THE INSTITUTIONAL TRAPS

The incremental government growth trap is the consequence of the nature of government growth. Government has not increased its power in great leaps forward. The actual history is less dramatic: sustained, incremental advances, usually desired by the electorate, and often desirable in themselves on social criteria. Generally the advance of government has been to correct a public bad or provide a public good.[5] Opposition has been seen as inhumane or mean, motivated by selfishness and indifference to human suffering, or by over-concern with small increases in government expenditure. But over time the sum of many small interventions has become one large intervention.

And when should the process stop? The desirability of any particular intervention has not been measured at the time of its implementation, in terms of its financial cost against the total cost of all interventions, or its

[5] "Public goods" (like defence and art galleries) and "public bads" (like industrial smog and vandalism) have the following characteristics: (a) they cannot be confined to individual ownership; the more of the good there is for one person, the more there is for other people; (b) the actual benefit (or loss) derived by any individual from the good, therefore, depends on how much of the good there is in the economy.

opportunity cost against alternative uses of resources. The apparently desirable and innocuous character of incremental advances in government masks a mounting tide of government, a "creeping socialism", insidious in its gradualness, and difficult to reverse because of the interests it creates. At no time is the total of interventions—the whole package of state goods—explicitly examined and put to electoral test, except in a very general way. General elections tend to be fought on particular incremental advances of government; electors are usually motivated by interest in specific existing benefits, or in proposed new benefits. Individuals, therefore, see the state through incremental blinkers which distort their vision, focussing attention on the particular and blurring the general. Not that individual action is necessarily irrational. Government in the long run is certainly a public bad, and as such poses the usual problems of externalities[6] and "free riders".[7] While it is in the interest of all individuals to restrain the growth of government and to reduce its size, it is not in the interest of any particular individual in the short run to work for restraint or reduction, if that action means an immediate loss of benefits. And most people benefit in some way from the actions of government, at least in the short run. Government growth seen incrementally, therefore, becomes acceptable; it becomes an almost

[6] An "externality" is that "neighbourhood effect" on third parties caused by the production, consumption or exchange activities of any individual. These effects can be beneficial or harmful. Nearly all economic activities have external effects.

[7] A "free rider" is an individual who benefits, without contributing, from a good or service produced by others. Collective action can produce a good or service (e.g., a park) which even those who do not contribute can enjoy.

involuntary process, avoiding critical scrutiny and building support as it advances. In this way, intervention has become a social habit.

THE PUBLIC INQUIRY TRAP

If the process of government growth has been incremental, the cause of growth has been public inquiry. Put simply: public inquiry into social problems leads to public solution of social problems. This is the public inquiry trap, a legacy of the 19th century when there was a transition from a largely private to a public view of social problems. The main mechanism whereby this change was accomplished was the parliamentary committee or the royal commission of inquiry set up by Parliament.

From early in the century, a process of the public (that is, governmental) remedy of 'social problems' was established in five stages:

first, the identification of a social problem by a group of reformers who publicise the problem;

second, as a result of the publicity, the setting-up of a committee of inquiry (often a House of Commons Committee), which gathers evidence, interviews witnesses, and writes a report with legislative recommendations;

third, the passing of remedial legislation;

fourth, the establishment of a bureaucracy of inspection and control, with delegated powers;

fifth, a feedback, whereby those who administer the law recommend further legislation.

The last stage was particularly important. The administrators, the civil servants, the specialists in social problems, came to know more about social problems than anybody else, and spoke with authority about the need to maintain, and often to extend, government intervention. These were often men of ferocious goodness, convinced of, and convincing in, the demands for intervention. The whole process was partly checked in the 19th century by a prevailing faith in *laissez-faire,* and by a Treasury view of national finance which began with the revenue side of the budget, not the expenditure side, and which argued that money was more productive in private than in government pockets.[8] But both these restraints lapsed in the 20th century, with declining faith in *laissez-faire,* and, increasingly, an expenditure view of public finance. This process went along with the belief, largely the result of the inquiry process outlined above, that all social problems were public problems and that all public problems were capable of solution by political means. The end of *laissez-faire* marked not only a declining belief in the efficiency of market economy, but disbelief also in the ability of individuals to deal with their personal problems, or even perhaps to understand them. At the same time public inquiries proliferated, so that now practically nothing that exists or occurs in society is not subjected to periodic large-scale investigation, and to continuous inspection and scrutiny. As inquiry has extended, so has government.

THE BUREAUCRATIC TRAP

If government grew incrementally but surely by assuming the roles of public inquirer, problem solver,

---

[8] This process is discussed in J. M. Buchanan, John Burton, Richard E. Wagner, *The Consequences of Mr Keynes*, Hobart Paper 78, IEA, 1978.

monitor of social ills and provider of social goods,[9] its manifest form was the increasing bureaucracy. The bureaucratic trap is the ability of bureaucracies to be self-perpetuating and self-enlarging,[10] always to grow and never to decline, to establish themselves so powerfully that they become a formidable interest group in society.

The dynamic for bureaucratic expansion is both external and internal. The external dynamic is provided by the continuous demand for increasing government from a wide variety of sources: from the socialist who wants state ownership of the means of production, to the defender of some small interest who sees effective support only in government. The demands for the extension of government today are formidable, and each demand implies an expansion of bureaucracy. If a century ago it was widely believed that intervention was undesirable in a free society, today it is widely believed that intervention is desirable, even if the cost is diminished freedom.

Bureaucracies grow not only because of external demand but because of an internal logic of expansion. Bureaucracies consist of "entrepreneurs in government", who naturally act with self-interest and in the interesst of "the firm" for which they work. They work, therefore, to enlarge their own interests, and the interests of "the firm"; they try to extend their responsibilities, because on this depends their immediate status and

[9] A "social good" is a good or service provided by government; it may mean a "public good" in the way defined above, but it has come to mean also anything that the government thinks it should provide.

[10] *The Economics of Politics,* Readings 18, IEA, 1978.

salary, and to enlarge the responsibilities of "the firm", because the larger "the firm", the greater the managerial opportunities. For these reasons bureaucracies always grow and never decline, and at a critical point of size become a powerful voting lobby in the societies they increasingly control. Their continued progress is then very difficult to stop.

V
CAN WE ESCAPE?

Can we escape? By 1989 or sooner, or not at all? Do entrenched interests—intellectual, bureaucratic, governmental and political—make escape, if not impossible, then, at best, unlikely? Is there still hope? I think there is.

The analysis above suggests actions which could free us from the public trap into which we have fallen. In general hope lies in the civilised arts of persuasion and debate to change attitudes, but in the long run changed attitudes must also be reflected in effective political action. And that means governments making decisions which at present would certainly be unpopular, and at any time could harm particular interests, but which, with changing attitudes, could become acceptable to a majority of the electorate. What, then, can be done to change attitudes? Let me suggest a series of specific actions, each intended to make escape from a particular trap possible; together they could give impetus to an effective demand for the reduction of government.

ESCAPING FROM THE TRAPS
From the social science trap, escape will be easier if there is widespread recognition of the failure of govern-

ments to achieve what they try to achieve, and wide-spread knowledge of the unintended and often unfortunate consequences of their actions. When the impossibility of social engineering is recognised, much of the uncritical faith in government will be destroyed. Action, therefore, should be directed towards revealing the inefficiency and ineffectiveness of government, always underlining its achievements in contrast with its claims, and always emphasising its failures in management and planning. It will be helpful both to question the ability of the social sciences to provide practical guidance for social policy and to re-assert the claims of history as a guide to the understanding of social organisation and social change.

From the activist intellectual trap, escape will be helped by publicising the role of the intellectuals in modern society, and their predominant interventionist ethic. In particular there should be awareness of *"la trahison des clercs"*—the treason of the intellectuals against freedom—by making explicit their élitist claims and their ambitions for power, their self-interested support of strong government, and their confusion between analysis and prescription, between the positive or analytically neutral and the normative or ethically prejudiced. It must be made quite clear that the intellectuals have no special claim to govern, or, indeed, that they have any special understanding of society that gives them authority to prescribe conduct in that society.

From the incremental governmental growth trap, escape will be possible only by developing an attitude towards government that always begins with the aggregate and not with the incremental; with the total of government interventions and not with any proposed increment; with the total of government expenditure and employment and not with the expenditure-employment effects of a particular intervention. When people begin to think of government in this way and to realise just how much of society's wealth and income is in its hands, and when people begin also to think of government, not as an abstract entity, but as consisting of individuals (politicians and civil servants), they will be sceptical about the growth of government, and particularly about the increasing concentration of power in the hands of those politicians and civil servants. People should be encouraged not to use the word "government" but instead to say "politicians and bureaucrats", making explicit just where power resides in a society in which government is large and growing.

From the public inquiry trap escape is particularly difficult, and can come, effectively, only from government action. But such action will be helped by trying to make civil servants more accountable, both in terms of the efficiency of the enterprises they run and of the administrative power they exercise over individual citizens. The power of bureaucrats should be publicised and criticised, along with their considerable privileges. In the long run, when opinions have changed, consideration should be given to disenfranchising, or partly disenfranchising, civil servants, on the grounds that their interests and privileges prejudice their objectivity as regards the power and extent of government.

All these suggestions for action have one element in common, the need for an active, voluntary and continuous criticism of government which will make clear to as large a proportion of the population as possible that they are in a public trap, but that escape is still possible. We still have some freedoms, and some choices. Those who believe in freedom must work for it. The costs are high, but the rewards are great. 1989 will not necessarily be 1984.

PART III

POLITICS AND PUBLIC POLICY

Politics and Public Policy

THE WORKER AND THE SOCIAL WAGE

Raymond Fletcher, MP

The Author

RAYMOND FLETCHER was born in 1921 and educated at University College, Nottingham. He has been Member of Parliament for Ilkeston since 1964. During 1974-76 he was Vice-President, Assembly of Council of Europe, Leader, UK Delegation to Council of Europe and WEU; Leader, Socialist Group in Council of Europe. He is a member of the Transport and General Workers' Union. Former columnist on *The Times*, contributor to journals at home and abroad, and author of *Sixty Pounds a Second on Defence* (1963).

The Worker and the Social Wage

The characteristics of an organisation, like those of a person, are largely determined in its infancy. This explains why the British Labour Party is different from most other parties in the Socialist International and why, for example, in most of the discussions that take place between European Socialists, the British are almost invariably the odd men out.

Its uniqueness was once a source of mild arrogance. In no other country than Britain, it was argued, was the party actually based on the trade unions and mainly financed by them. In no other country was the party so organically linked with trade unionists that there was no danger of the Labour Party dwindling, as had some Continental parties, into coteries of academics with no organisation and therefore no capacity to win votes and office.

There were other differences, but the one relevant to the theme of this paper is the attitude of the Labour Party towards the state and the market economy.

LABOUR, THE STATE AND THE MARKET—NO ORIGINAL ANTIPATHY

The party has never paid much attention to theory. The Webbs were revered—but by a Labour movement they despised. Professor R. H. Tawney, who managed to be a good man as well as a good historian, attracted awe; but the practical Labour Party members read their manuals of election organisation more diligently than *Religion and the Rise of Capitalism*. Evan Durbin might have given the party a scholarly set of reasons for existing (the only function, I regret to say, of the political theorist in Britain) but did not live long enough to do so. Bernard Shaw, of course, pranced around; but his ideas, encapsulated in his preface to *The Perfect Wagnerite*, were so frighteningly and cold-bloodedly totalitarian that even Wagner's own pamphlets, bad as they were, are preferable as tracts for reformers. They were at least written by a human being (though most of the admirers of his music would have found it difficult to refrain from punching him on the jaw had they met him). H. G. Wells's first contribution to British socialist thought, *Anticipations*, is a frightful book; and nobody in the British Labour Party could have gained much from a work that resembles *Mein Kampf* in so many passages.

Other Socialist parties produced intellectual giants like Karl Kautsky, who would write a whole volume to clear his mind on one item in the German Social Democratic Party's programme, or Rudolf Hilferding, who predicted the coming of the European Community half a century before it arrived. Jean Jaures, the pre-1914 French Socialist leader, wrote a history of the French Revolution which is still taken seriously by scholars. Thought and scholarship, as well as indignation, went into Continental Socialism.

The only British socialist writer who won fame, and a large readership, by writing about socialism was Robert Blatchford. But he paid no attention to the nuts-and-bolts problems of changing a social and economic order. Like all English revolutionaries (and especially the effective ones of the 17th century), Blatchford looked backwards for his Utopia—to an England wherein the common people had ceased to work in ugly, unhealthy factories for the profit of heartless, over-affluent absentee employers. The maypole dance was a more suitable symbol of his attitudes than a planning directive, and it is hardly surprising that he was intensely patriotic and that his best-known work should be entitled *Merrie England.*

This country, it is obvious, was hardly boiling with socialist intellectual ferment when the Labour Party was coming into existence. Yet there was a ferment of feeling, and what is significant about this feeling is that it did not (as Fascism was to do twenty years later) centre on the state, still less glorify it; and it did not spill over into a rejection of the market as such.

The market came into it, of course. But a condemnation of the fact that Lord Tomnoddy, the coal owner, had five hundred times as much purchasing power to bring to the market as his employee, Mr Henry Dubb, the coal-miner, is no basis for a condemnation of the market mechanism, any more than the fact that Sir Henry Dubb, the property dealer, who does not care for opera, can afford to go to Covent Garden more often than I, who love it, should be the starting point of an argument against presenting opera at Covent Garden at all. In the eyes of the early Labour supporters, it was the contrast between too much money at one end of the social scale and too little at the other that was villainous, not the measuring instrument which demonstrated that difference—and the market is no more than a measuring instrument, just like a set of scales or a thermometer.

THE 1920s—MORRISON *v.* ENGELS

It is true that the idea of the common ownership of the means of production and exchange rose to the surface and eventually found its way into the Labour Party constitution in the famous Clause IV. But it was not until the 1920s that common ownership and state ownership met and married. Herbert Morrison was the marriage broker, but a much more formidable socialist, Friedrich Engels, was so far removed from the Morrisonian concept that, towards the end of his life, he hailed the limited liability (or joint-stock) company as a potentially socialist institution. Karl Marx, of course, was a state-smasher if there ever was one, and even looked forward to the withering away of that part of the state machinery that the revolution had not demolished. The market, to him, was merely an instrument of economic life.

Why, then, did hostility to the gross inequalities which the market reflected and, in those days, magnified gradually transform itself into hostility to the market as such? Two words provide the answer—slumps and unemployment. It would carry me beyond the bounds set for this essay to go deeper into the connection between markets and misery as the early socialist theorists saw it. What does keep me on the tracks is the assertion that this view was, so to speak, part of the foundation stone on which the doctrine of state ownership and state direction was laid.

Another part of the foundation stone, fashioned as much by liberals as by socialists, was the grinding poverty which even economic booms seemed unable to remove. Charity merely touched its surface. Trade unionism, at that time beginning to feel and show its muscles, was unable to pull the very poor people, about whom Jack London had written so eloquently, out of the abyss he had described in one of his most widely-read books.

BISMARCKIAN 'STATE SOCIALISM'

There was only one answer, it seemed. And it was found, not in the theories of socialists or the humane impulses of Liberals and social reformers, but in the practice of that master of cynical statecraft, Bismarck. It was the Iron Chancellor who had nationalised the German railways to strengthen the German state and the anti-socialist creator of the German Empire who introduced state insurance to take the wind out of the sails of the growing social-democratic party (a Marxist one at that time). The old schemer was no hypocrite. He even called his system *Staatssocialismus* to make it quite clear what he was doing.

But his intervention—an effective one by 19th-century standards—into the poverty-abolition business brings into the argument not only another paradox (a Prussian *Junker* injecting more socialism into Imperial Germany than all the socialists and trade unionists of Britain were able to in the traditional home of social progress!). It also brought another illustration of the proposition that socialism and the state were not always in love with one another. His use of the term *Staats-socialismus* implied that state socialism was better than the anarchy and disruptiveness then associated with real socialism.

It has been necessary, however tiresome to economists, to take this quick trip into history in order to validate one proposition. Much of what will be attacked by other contributors to this symposium, and a political attitude which is about to be repudiated by me, was not planned by any party or organisation. It just grew. Institutions were created as what seemed at the time of their creation a necessary response to the challenge of a specific problem—whether it was that of poverty in the 1890s or the state of the coal industry in the 1940s. Nearly everybody who did anything at all added a few bricks to the structure of the state during the last three-quarters of a century. All political parties have, to coin an ugly word, gone in for "statification"; and it should be possible, therefore, to subdue the party passions that burst into most arguments and offer statements as coldly clinical as a surgeon's analysis of a set of X-rays. We have all let what was planned as a landscape grow into a jungle.

THE 'SOCIAL WAGE'/'SALARY'/'INCOME'

All of which brings me to what practically every other socialist treats as a sacred cow, and which I regard in much the same light as the real holy, underfed animals of India, which the poor peasants of that country would be much better off without. I am referring to the "social wage". This, in the words of a famous House of Commons' Motion, has increased, is increasing and ought to be diminished.

The term "social wage" has, of course, had its meaning distorted since it began to be used as political ammunition. Since it describes those goods and services which are provided "free" to the consumer, whether as

medical attention, his children's education or subsidies
for both council house rent-payers and the payers-off
of mortgages, but paid for by the whole community
almost wholly by taxation (the national insurance
contribution pays for only a fraction of health care and
unemployment benefit), "social salary" or "social
income" would be equally applicable. The word "wage"
implies that only manual or blue-collar workers receive
it. This is quite wrong. We all do. And that is what is
wrong for a start.

Naturally, nobody can possibly object to paying, by
taxation, for assistance to disabled or chronically sick
fellow-citizens. There are many other unfortunates to
whom I am prepared to give aid either *via* the Chancellor
or through charities. But why should others be taxed to
pay part of the interest on my mortgage, if I had one?
Most of those who pay need the money more than I
need the tax relief.

Successive governments have defended glaring anom-
alies like this on various grounds. One wants to see a
"property-owning democracy" and therefore gives
financial relief to house purchasers. Another, concerned
with raising the living standards of working-class
tenants, lowers their rents by subsidy. Laudable aims of
well-intentioned men and women, without doubt, but
how often are they actually achieved by the means
adopted to realise them?

There is a difference between going to Joe Bloggs,
who cannot get a good job because of a pit accident
some years ago, and giving him something (either by
reduced rent or direct payment) to enable him and his
family to buy good food and take a good holiday, and
showering subsidies on every tenant in the country just

to make sure that Mr Bloggs is a little better off. Medical Officers of Health do not insist that everyone in their areas be given chest medicines because two extra cases of bronchitis have been reported in one village.

So with mortgage interest relief. Most socialist supporters in the country want to own their own houses and see nothing wrong in helping young Henry Bloggs, married two weeks ago, to get a house for himself and his wife. If this means letting him start to pay for it without paying a deposit or giving him a low-interest loan, what is wrong with that? But why give me any assistance if I want to buy a house?

The underlying justification, irrespective of the colour of the governments which can find no way of helping someone without distributing largesse to nearly everyone, is that these are redistributive and therefore democratising measures. So they might be if the Shah of Iran or the King of Saudi Arabia footed the bill for them. Yet even if they did, the effects of taxation undo any redistributive element in the measures themselves. Equalising through taxing and subsidising probably works on the graphs they once had in the London School of Economics. In real life, among real people, they do not. I have no need to fill two pages with statistics. Ask any MP what complaints take up most of his time at his weekly surgery. Most of the moans and groans that reach him are about the unfair consequences of legislation intended to spread fairness all round. To put it bluntly, there is really no such thing as a "social wage": there is a movement of goods, services and money into households and a corresponding movement of taxes out. Roughly speaking, what is received as benefit is paid for as tax—by the recipients.

I do not propose to pepper this essay with statistics, first, because when one is arguing for a change of emphasis in one strand of political thought and a change of direction in the policies that derive from it, lists of figures frequently obscure what they are intended to illustrate. Secondly, the necessary arithmetic has already been done quite recently by Mr Arthur Seldon in his provocative book *Charge*.[1]

But statistics confirm what common sense has long since established. In one of his broadcasts from the United States, Mr Alistair Cooke asked an Italian pre-1914 immigrant what he had learned from 60 years of living in the most affluent country on earth. The old man pondered for a bit and then came out with the one proposition in economics that is quite irrefutable. "There's no such thing," said the old chap, "as a free lunch." Nor is there any such thing as a free health service, free education or free assistance with improving your house. Society does not generate funds out of nowhere which public authority gives away according to need. Nor are the rich made compulsory donors to the poor. There are not enough of the former and too many of the latter.

Poverty is a relative term. The poorest family in my constituency lives in a way that even Queen Elizabeth I would envy in some respects. The condition, therefore, will always be with us and, unless the body politic regresses and becomes as callous an organism as the Todt Organisation, which controlled slave labour under

[1] Maurice Temple Smith, 1977. Mr Seldon does not carry me with him down every path he explores. But he goes on his economic explorations with the aim of improving the living standards and earnings of working people (which puts us in the same camp at the start).

the Nazis, the prosperous will be obligated to do something to alleviate it.

The housing problem, too, will never be "solved". Houses decay. The expectations of the house-seeker continually rise. So will the cost of building a house, or even modernising one. The question is: will the expansion of the social wage reduce the two problems so that, at least, the sum total of deprivation in the community goes down?

It might. Nothing seems impossible in a world where machines can be fitted with simple brains—the silicon-chip computers—and cars made in factories with no more than half a dozen human beings in sight. Yet so long as people are free there are bounds set to what either governments or scientists can do to them. (Even the totalitarian states do not exercise the almost total control exercised by those who created them. Comrade Stalin could do practically anything he wanted. Comrade Brezhnev, though the most powerful military leader in the world, cannot.)

DIFFERENTIALS *v.* DEPENDENCE ON THE STATE

The limits to the social wage are set when trade union conferences assemble to formulate their annual set of demands. At one time those demands would have been as much for action by the state as for higher wages from the employers. Now most of the debates will be centred on wages (increase of) and taxes (reduction of). Any government minister who throws in the social wage as a reason for moderating demands for wages in the wallet will be listened to politely—and ignored. Unions may moderate their wage demands, and they may do it for political reasons. But the social wage will not be a dominant influence on their thinking—if, indeed, it is now strong at all.

In short, the Labour movement which accepted the social wage, and the state which distributed it, as instruments of social progress and even as a painless path to socialism, are beginning to throw off the heritage of the Webbs. It is true that it is a slow-moving movement. But it is equally true that a great shift of emphasis, hardly noticed yet by those who made it, has taken place. The trade unionist, despite the exaggerated fears of the Duke of Edinburgh, is becoming more of an individual, arguing at conferences about differentials rather than increasing his dependence on the state. Fringe benefits do not, as the Duke asserts, diminish the stature of those who negotiate for and receive them. He should look at the experience of the US, where fringe benefits feature prominently in the impassioned disputes that precede the signing of every contract between enterprises and unions. A fringe benefit, *negotiated by those who receive it, is a substitute for the social wage, not a re-named form of it.*

I am no uncritical apologist for trade unions. But the noisy, nauseating, over-publicised rabble-rousers should not be regarded as the trade union movement. They are excrescences, not the essence; and their rise to prominence occurred because the unions themselves were confused and apathetic—and seemingly robbed of the main reason for existing at all, which was negotiating better wages and working conditions.

The lurch away from traditional trade union aims is ending, as I predicted it would when the revolt against the "militant" shop stewards took place at Longbridge. But as trade unions turn back to being trade unions their leaders will discover what so many of their members already know. Choice is becoming the invisible, desirable increment to cash in the working-class family. And choice, once it becomes possible, is widened by those now in a position to make it.

When I first went to my present constituency, workers went to work on buses. Now they have cars, and, I am told by car dealers, they choose them with discrimination. Two decades ago the miners I represent went to boarding houses in Skegness for their holidays. Now they go down to travel agents (and it is significant that the best one in my area is run by a co-operative society) and discuss the relative merits of Rimini and Sorrento. Working-class housewives naturally have as much say in these matters as their husbands. No wonder! A score of labour-saving devices in the kitchen and twice that number in the rest of the house have liberated women more effectively than any Commission set up to do so; and the social wage, except in one form, plays no role in this process at all.

Ordinary workers who have never read a line of mine —or of Arthur Seldon's—will whittle down the social wage, first because it costs too much in taxes, and, secondly, because they have entered into the realm of choice—and they like it. (I should add that this is a description of a trend already with us, not a prediction.) Owing to a prolonged illness I was able to spend a good deal of the year 1977 walking around my constituency (a predominantly working-class one which has returned Labour MPs since 1922, with the exception of 1931-35 when a McDonald supporter won it by two votes), talking to constituents. My view of the future is less dismal than the Duke of Edinburgh's because it is a distillation of a thousand conversations.

But back to the social wage. In one form, I maintained, it was likely to remain. I refer, of course, to the National Health Service.

FINANCIAL ANAEMIA OF THE NHS

It is true that, as workers and working-class organisations increase their stake in the existing system and, therefore, their incomes from it, they might go for insurance rather than taxation—or a German-type mixture of the two—but they will certainly support some cure for the financial anaemia afflicting the NHS.

As to their capacity to do so, from choice, it is permissible to assume that a social trend that has emerged in the United States will also come to the surface here. It is a social change as great as any envisaged by the early socialists, but it has taken place subterraneously.

Put in a sentence it is that, through their pension funds, American workers now own at least 25 per cent of the equity capital of American business and, by 1985, will own at least 40—if not 60—per cent of such capital. The 1,000 largest pension funds already have virtual control (i.e. one-third of the capital) of nearly all of the 1,000 largest American corporations.[2]

It is a paradox that appeals to me—the man from the Pru being the unwitting agent of social revolution, workers' control and all that. Yet though the American experience is unlikely to be repeated exactly over here, there are one or two indications that trade union attitudes towards the investment of union money are changing. The railwaymen's pension fund, for example, owns a valuable art collection.

[2] Peter F. Drucker, *The Unseen Revolution*, Heinemann, 1976.

Given fair winds—that is, the assumption that our society will simmer down into order and our economy pull itself upwards into increased productivity—attitudes will inevitably change. The worker will not become bourgeois (whatever that may mean). But his resistance to some charges for his health care will inevitably lessen if such resistance is demonstrably reducing both the quality and quantity of such care.

The architects of the Health Service, notably the late Aneurin Bevan, worked on the fallacious assumption that once the health problems that were a legacy of the previous two or three decades had been dealt with, the Service would gradually shift its emphasis from cure to prevention and, so to speak, cut itself down to size as the general health of the population improved. Better feeding, better housing and a health-promoting environment would slowly reduce the demand for medical treatment.

In fact, the opposite happened and continues to happen, and the Service, with its open-ended commitment to provide treatment, lives in crisis and, in certain vital areas such as mental health, only just manages to survive at all. In the present situation (vastly different from that foreseen in 1948), it is quite clear that some form of control must be imposed on both supply and demand and it is equally clear that the present method of cutting back by the Department is as clumsy as using a circular saw to remove a corn.

Charges are already imposed for prescriptions, even though they are purely nominal. But there are other charges, less well-known. Pensioners, for example, are charged a kind of hotel fee after a certain period in hospital. Nobody else is, apart from the dwindling number of private patients. The principle of "free" treatment, therefore, has already been breached.

So why should it be thought horrendous to suggest that charges be imposed by general practitioners for out-of-hours calls? Or that the torrents of largely useless medicine poured down patients' throats (the phrase, incidentally, comes from Bevan) be checked by charging? I will not list other ways in which the Service can get more funds. This is not an essay on the National Health Service. The proposition advanced is that the citizen is increasingly able and increasingly willing to pay for more things like wine and cigarettes. He expects neither to be part of the social wage. So why should he jib at paying something for his medical attention? And what principle is violated if he is asked to?

Whenever I have had to admit that I have believed in or supported nonsense I have always pleaded that it seemed a good idea at the time. The social wage was a good idea at the time. Beveridge and Bevan were neither idiots nor incipient totalitarians.

But times have changed in ways that hardly anyone anticipated three decades ago. Politics, as I have said, is the realm of paradox; and the usual consequences of legislation are the precise opposite of those intended. In calling for the phasing out of most of the social wage I am merely recognising this, and moving in the real world of my constituents instead of the ideal one I inhabited for so long.

What is important is that it is the working-class recipients of the social wage who now want it replaced, and their numbers are growing. They can do their arithmetic. They like choice and, to an increasing extent, can afford it. A Labour movement that gives it to them, whether in the form of negative income tax (which I was advocating some years ago) or in some other way, will not lose their support. It will not be the heritage of Bevin and Bevan that is being jettisoned. It will be that of Bismarck.

THE LONG, HARD ROAD OF REFORM

The road of reform is always long and frequently hard. Once it is embarked on, moreover, interests (real or imaginary) build themselves into obstacles, passions centre themselves on the obstacles and what is being attempted is totally obscured by the exchange of insults and bullets, according to whether one lives in a relatively free or an almost ossified society.

Most of the aims of the French Revolution, for example, were achieved—at least as far as intentions were concerned—in a few hours on that famous Versailles tennis court. Yet it took 26 years of conflict, with another spasm in 1830, before France enjoyed some liberty, a certain amount of equality and a modicum of fraternity.

British history offers a sackful of examples. Sir Robert Peel got his policemen more than a century after the need for them had become glaringly obvious. Women got the vote over three centuries after Elizabeth I had demonstrated not only that a woman could rule but could do it better than any monarch who had occupied the British throne. Less spectacular reforms also ran a gauntlet of passionate and ignorant opposition. We could not afford Shaftesbury. We could not afford Plimsoll. We could not afford either Churchill or Lloyd George. Such is the encapsulated history of British reform: reforms generate revolutions; the country cannot afford them; and the beneficiaries of reform are too stupid or degraded to worry about anyway.

Why should it be any different this time, not only with the very modest reforms suggested in this paper, but others? There is no reason at all, of course. Mass education, far from producing a new Age of Reason, seems to have done quite the opposite. No 19th-century newspaper editor would have printed either horoscopes or soft pornography. Today the popular newspapers print anything—a bit of news, true, but usually in a big headlined spread with a few paragraphs of news thrown in to fill up the page. Only three newspapers print anything like adequate reports of what is actually said in Parliament or printed in Government documents. A demagogue could perhaps break through this. But what demagogue has ever been a rational reformer? Hitler? Eva Peron? No: the first reaction to the idea of putting more money (and therefore more choice) into people's pockets will be the demagogic howl that something is being taken away. That is the first obstacle.

INSTITUTIONAL AND UNION RESISTANCES

The second is the institutionalised one. There are thousands engaged in the administration of the distribution of the social wage. They are almost invariably honest, good people who see no other way of alleviating poverty; and the alleviation—I would say the "abolition" were it not a relative term—of poverty is an aim we all share. Yet these good people, having known only one way of doing it, will stoutly resist any other—and anyone who imagines that a Minister runs his Department in the same way as a captain his ship knows nothing of politics. Institutional resistance from civil servants is going to be powerful and could be decisive.

The third is the trade unions. Here, where one would expect to confront an obstacle fashioned from Chobham steel, I see signs that are, as I have hinted above, encouraging. A reform that enables them to raise wages, which is what they are for, but ensures that the old, the sick and the disabled are not penalised thereby could be sold to the trade unions by reason and persuasion. There are naturally certain pre-conditions for such an exercise. The economy must be healthy, the value of the currency stable, and the reforms presented as structural changes in a system which will continue to fulfil the first proposition advanced by Mr Arthur Seldon in *Charge*: "all people should have the minimum essentials for civilised living". In other words, a great change must be presented as no change at all, *and everyone should feel it to be beneficial after the inevitable teething troubles.* If the italicised condition is not met there will be no change.

It is to the Labour movement that most of my arguments are addressed. First of all, I belong to it and have no intention of leaving it. Secondly, it represents most of the interests behind the continuation of the social wage in its present form. Thirdly (and rather pathetically), I hope to convince it that the very changes it has brought about in living standards and expectations now require a change in its attitude towards society which in no way conflicts with what the early socialists taught that socialism was all about.

A political party is a tool and only for a few fanatics a way of life. A carpenter will put aside a blunted chisel and take up a sharp one. Millions of working-class people will put aside the Labour Party if it continues to be associated with armies of bureaucrats, mountains of paper and high tax demands.

If the party does not change, people will change. In California they have just staged a tax "strike". (That is the word for it though it was done perfectly constitutionally by referendum under State law.) It could happen, unconstitutionally, here. The miners, after all, did not worry about constitutional niceties when they struck in support of a justifiable wage claim in February 1974. Any politician who imagines that the British people are sheep all the time is heading for trouble.

REFORM VIA REVERSE INCOME TAX:
A NATIONAL CREDIT CARD SYSTEM?

So how do we make the changes? The first thing I would suggest is that everyone fills in a new kind of income return, similar to a tax return but much simpler. This would provide a code number. Some codes would carry an entitlement to certain free services and monetary payments to the really disadvantaged. The code number could, in order to remove every vestige of that detested word (detested, that is, among working-class people) "charity", be embossed on a credit card.

This national credit card system would operate in the same way as any other. A disabled pensioner, for instance, would sign her rent book, the collector would check the card signature and that would be that. The same for rates, the same for the purchase of appliances, the same for the payment of home helps and so on. As far as income tax was concerned her code would indicate that she was entitled to a reverse income tax of £x and she would receive that instead of a demand. Her pension would be paid by cheque. Her card would pay for medical and dental care. The reverse, or negative, income tax system has been so much discussed that there is no need to argue its merits here.

There is, in fact, only one way to run major reforms through the barriers that are raised against them. It is to begin reforming in a modest way, get the first instalment accepted and then allow popular demands for the removal of snags and the improvement of the new system to provide the momentum for further change. Society, in short, given the incentive, will change itself. It always has.

Politics and Public Policy

THE POINT OF NO RETURN?

Jo Grimond, MP

The Author

JO GRIMOND was born in 1913 and educated at Eton and Balliol College, Oxford. He has been Member of Parliament for Orkney and Shetland since 1950 and was Leader of the Parliamentary Liberal Party, 1956-67, and May-July 1976. Chancellor of the University of Kent at Canterbury since 1970. Director of the Manchester Guardian and Evening News since 1967. Author of *The Liberal Future* (1959); *The Liberal Challenge* (1963); (with B. Neve) *The Referendum* (1975); *The Common Welfare* (1978). Contributor to *The Prime Ministers* (1976); *My Oxford* (1977). For the IEA he contributed a paper, "Trade Unions Harm the Poor", in *Trade Unions: Public Goods or Public 'Bads'?* (Readings 17, 1978), and "Introductory Remarks" in *The Economics of Politics* (Readings 18, 1978).

The Point of No Return?

The "public" (a euphemism for *government*) sector is not founded on organic human evolution. It grows for different reasons. It may soon be reaching a point of no return when freedom and efficiency, investment and the incentive to work are so condemned that only a dictatorship could keep the country even at a painfully low standard of living.

Liberals accept the dangers of original sin but believe that individuals by themselves are capable of running a good society.

TOO MUCH GOVERNMENT

The history of human government recognises that some restraint on liberty is essential in the light of original sin, but it warns of the appalling effects of too much government. This is indeed the classic dilemma between freedom and order. Freedom should mean the freedom of a free, impartial order under the law. Freedom still sometimes means the arbitrary tyranny of the dictator.

This view of men in society was held by liberal democrats and is the tradition that runs through Locke, Burke, Hume, Adam Smith, John Stuart Mill and the other Scottish political philosophers and economists down, say, to the American Walter Lippmann in our time. Though this philosophy is individualist in that it believes that values reside in the individual and not in an abstraction, though it therefore believes in liberty and opportunity for the individual to express himself, it does not believe that the individual subsists on his (or her) own. It believes that what is important in human society is the interplay between individuals and the actions and reactions of the community. Government is the instrument by which the community supplies services like the police. It is not the only means which the community has of ordering its affairs. Once government assumes it is the origin of political power and—in the name of religion, communism, superior knowledge or the "right" of majorities or of interest-groups, trade unions or bureaucracies—tries to over-ride the community, tyranny is close at hand.

BIGGER GOVERNMENT IS NOT BEAUTIFUL

For most of history government has been regarded as an evil, even though a necessary evil. Edmund Burke said government was a contrivance of human wisdom to satisfy human want. If the human race was to live in peace and be able to improve its lot, save, invest and create wealth, it had to co-operate to discharge some functions. But the notion that bigger government is better government is contrary to all experience. It is astonishing not that modern government works badly but that anyone should think it would work at all. To entrust government with more and more power—indeed, to beseech it to take more—might seem in the light of history a sign of madness.

The Founding Fathers of the USA, true children of the 18th-century enlightenment, were under no illusions about the corrupting effects of power. They devised a constitution which ensured that the executive was curbed and balanced. Their heirs in Europe and perhaps even in America are forgetting the age-old lessons of the history of politics.[1]

LAW AND THE MARKET

The liberals of the first half of the 19th century saw that there should be two systems anterior to government: the rule of law and the market economy. Both were ways in which the community were kept together. Both enabled individuals in the community to use their talents, both were guarantees of freedom, both were guarantees of equality.

The rule of law sprang from the morality of the community. Morality by its nature is the same for all. All, therefore, in so far as they are moral beings, should be equal under the law. The growth of a secular morality strengthened the rule of law. From Immanuel Kant onwards through the 19th century the general interest and the general will were widely accepted with their moral imperatives such as the Golden Rule.

From the rule of law grew respect for constitutions. That Britain did not have a written constitution in the American style did not mean that her 19th-century statesmen were not deeply imbued by constitutional notions. What affronted Palmerston about European dictatorships was not the lack of a voting franchise: it was the lack of constitutional checks upon the autocracy. When Gladstone or Asquith wanted to make

[1] [Compare observations of Professor J. M. Buchanan in *The Economics of Politics*, Readings 18, IEA, 1978.—ED.]

changes in the method of government, a bare majority was not enough. They were almost as conscious as was Burke of the need to respect the organic growth of the body politic and take into account the various branches of the state.[2]

The free market enabled everyone in the community to exercise choice. That the choice of the poor was much smaller than that of the rich was all too true. But the choice of the poor was even smaller in the time of mercantilism. The free market allowed for the distribution of resources according to demand. It contributed to a vastly increased output of cheap and sought-after goods. Further, not only has no other system allocated resources so well. Socialist systems in Eastern Europe have been compelled to fall back on it. Socialist planning with no free market will not work.

The Founding Fathers of America, and those who thought along similar lines in Northern Europe, had good reason for optimism. America remains a miracle, approached only by Japan which, if the efficient output of material goods is to be the criterion, should be a model for all under-developed countries. Nor are Americans or North West Europeans disillusioned about the political and economic background of liberal democracy. In spite of all the professed admiration of Communist countries, there is no rush to go there. The Russian record of creating human misery surpasses even the Nazis.

[2] [Compare the argument of Professor Gordon Tullock that for such constitutional change a bare simple majority is not sufficient and should be replaced by a two-thirds majority: *The Vote Motive*, Hobart Paperback 9, IEA, 1976.—ED.]

INDIVIDUAL DEVALUED: REPLACED BY GROUPS RUN BY BUREAUCRACIES

All is not well, nor ever will be. There is a high level of material well-being, freedom and education in the democracies, but also contradictions and difficulties. The rule of law and the market economy depend on a fairly general acceptance of morality which, in turn, depends on an appreciation of the organic nature of human society and a respect for the individual in it. But today in Britain the importance of men and women is more and more attached to their role: as members of a trade union, or a profession, civil servants, executives of a firm, or even as members of "the unemployed" or "the disabled". These organisations are run by bureaucracies whose main aim is to increase their empire and gain as much as they can in pay and resources. The "general interest"—the interest of the community— goes to the wall. Government is called more and more to intervene in particular situations instead of relying upon an impartial system. It is a reversion to the political situation in the Middle Ages and the Renaissance, when powerful barons and later powerful monied interests disputed the authority of the Crown or tried to use it for their own purposes. So it is in Britain today, much more than between, say, 1870 and 1914.

We must not assume that democracy in its more extreme form was advocated in either Britain or America. In Britain, consonant with the fear of too much government, the job of Parliament was largely negative. It was to question, criticise and thwart the executive.

"RULE OF THE JUNGLE": MARKET OR STATE PLANNING?

Contradictions between the political and economic systems have exposed the essential weaknesses of liberal democracy. For a period the presuppositions of a general interest, equality before the law, and the market economy were broadly accepted, and the system worked. But now the strike, or threat to strike, used not against the employer but against the public, has confounded the rule of law and the concept of an over-riding general interest. Not only the weekly wage-earner but also the civil servant and the white-collar worker look to their own interest—or what they believe it to be, though in the longer term all will suffer. And the market has been rendered much less effective.

The planners, in all parties, claimed that the market was "unscientific", that rational human beings should not be at the mercy of "blind" economic forces or the whim of millionaires or large companies. In a curious phrase, the market has been called the "rule of the jungle". That term describes not the market but much of socialist planning. For the rule of the jungle is the rule of the strongest—of the party which can either use the state machinery or industrial action.

Today in Britain we are indeed in a jungle where the strongest trade unions and bureaucracies grab what they can get. The planners, the people in control, are not free from the old vices which go with power. However repulsive some of the habits of the old-style millionaires may seem, there remains something in Dr Johnson's dictum that men are seldom so innocently employed as when making money. At least, power-seeking is worse. And the combination of the two is worst of all. The completely free operation of the market with its boom and slumps led to much human misery. The social services and public works were an attempt to alleviate it. The control of credit and Keynesian economics were also an attempt to meet it by general policies affecting the whole economy. But Parliament in Britain now exerts less power than the bureaucracy—which also dispenses vast patronage—or the unions.

POLITICAL BRIBERY

These general efforts in government alleviation were not sufficient to satisfy the bureaucratic urges in our society. So at every election political parties have to offer a programme of government action, which has become a series of bribes offered to particular bureaucracies or groups of voters. It is usually in conflict with the economic and general needs of the community in two respects.

First, the timing of politics is quite different from that of economics. Again and again government introduces measures which will take effect only when the situation has changed. Secondly, every programme of every party in Britain in recent years has meant more state intervention, more interference with the market, more of the national income taken by the state and more use of resources by the state. As production is hardly rising, and of what the public wants is not rising at all, the inevitable result is inflation and a growing loss of efficiency, partly through the ever-increasing number of non-producing bureaucrats and partly for lack of adequate incentive to efficiency in the "public" sector, where resources are wasted and misapplied.

The political democratic system in Britain, and I suspect in most of the Western world, is failing to cope with a situation for which its protagonists are not prepared. The origin and possible cure of the political problem is not understood. Our wastage of raw materials, our position *vis-à-vis* the under-developed countries, and the difficulties of our cities are caused by the very same type of thinking which made the atom bomb or put a man on the moon. Both are the result of deliberate governmental planning. Both are a waste of resources. Neither has anything to do with the general good or the free market. The most successful development of under-developed countries in terms of material resources is in the USA and Japan. The worst utilisation of vast resources is in state-planned Russia.

The difficulties of the cities are prime examples not of the free market but of constant public interference, constant increases in welfare at the expense of production, constant bad planning, the constant subsidisation of uneconomic activities. And by uneconomic I mean activities the public does not want to pay for.

HOW LONG CAN THE MARKET LAST?

Until recently the market was strong enough to bear the disturbances and impositions put upon it by politicians and bureaucrats. It is becoming doubtful how far this will remain true. Taxes, subsidies, public bodies have proliferated to such an extent that the economic nexus which regulates society is in danger of snapping. And at the same time as the bonds of the community are in danger of breaking, a high proportion of our ablest people are in futile, or at least unproductive and inessential, occupations.

If liberal democracy is to develop in the next hundred years its best features and shed its worst, three ideas must be accepted. The troubles are political or politico-economic. They stem from the growth of the bureaucratic attitude in all its forms, from the power of pressure groups, and from the resurgence of Communist absolutism. First, we must re-assert the primacy of the individual as a moral creature capable of developing his talents and making his choices within a community. We now see the pulverising effects of extreme economic or technological determinism treating human beings as monads to be manipulated either by a ruling bureaucracy or by inescapable laws. But in re-asserting the individual we must, second, emphasise the community. And, third, since the rule of law and the market have been so badly damaged, we must examine whether they can be resuscitated or replaced.

RESTORING LAW AND THE MARKET

The rule of law could be improved and extended by a Bill of Individual Rights. Since Home Rule for Scotland and Wales will require a written constitution, the opportunity could be taken to write into such fundamental documents protection for the generality of the community against vested interests.

And we must re-define the limits of the market. Very many human activities cannot be subject to the pure play of the market—though in most purely economic relationships it is the best regulator. It is also true that a system which gives interest-groups such political power to interfere with the market is inherently unstable. Most fundamental of all is the unequal start of boys and girls from different communities. The difficulty here, for reasons of morality as it affects both the community and the individual, is to reconcile scope for some accumulation and inheritance of private property with equality of opportunity. A striking feature is the wide gulf—in spite, indeed perhaps because, of high taxation, subsidies, regional development, etc—between the worst and the best areas. In his or her chances of education, health, jobs, housing or indeed capacity to cope with life, the child of the poorer areas is still far worse off than the child of the richer. In Britain the "social" services are largely personal services acting upon the individual only *after* he is in trouble. Though very expensive, their sights are set at reaching some minimum standard by centralised bureaucratic action. They neither do enough to improve the surroundings and thereby *prevent* misfortune, nor to involve the local community or the individuals concerned. Funds should be put at the disposal of local voluntary communities to develop their own way of life.

FREE ECONOMY AND WORK "PARTICIPATION"

In the economy there are two major questions to be tackled. Can a free economy run without much wider "participation" and ownership? Is not the inevitable result in a democracy that interest-groups use political means to twist the economy to their liking? We should certainly copy the German policies of wider participation, but what if the majority of workers do not want actively to participate? Are we not then faced with the possibility of companies being taken over by disruptive minority elements? The solution lies in distinguishing between the worker's wish to be kept informed, to have a right to express his opinion when he finds it necessary, and continual active participation in management, which is at best a long way off.

In Britain the motives of those who run nationalised industries are the same as those who run private enterprise. But nationalised industries are not subject to competition; they are inefficient, over-manned and wasteful of capital. The motives of their unions, or of those who advocate further nationalisation, are not public service but the assurance that taxpayers' money will keep them in their jobs for ever. Had the stagecoach industry been nationalised it would be going today. Equally, many in the so-called private sector behave very much as those in the public sector. But public monopolies are even more inefficient than private monopolies.

"PUBLIC" AND PRIVATE GOODS

What we must try to do is to disentangle once again the types of economic activity which are strictly "national" from those that are personal or individual. One of the most serious incursions of the state in liberal democracies is into voluntary work—though often from the best of motives. In our dislike of "charity" we are trying to run against some of the strongest of human instincts—to look after our families and neighbours.

When we move into the economic sphere it surely must be wrong to confine the market to the retail trades, betting, eating, drinking, and the production of luxury goods. "The public interest", that misused phrase, is served by efficiency. Efficiency is not a god to be worshipped but an instrument to be used. It has to be regulated by law and some of its products used for national and communal purposes. But all people are consumers. As consumers they want efficiency and cheapness.

In Britain, America and the Western world generally the public interest is best served by such firms as Marks & Spencer and their American equivalents, not by nationalised industries. The motor car has brought problems, but the pleasure it has given is tremendous. If you compare the development of the motor industry with that of the aircraft industry, dominated by motives of prestige, bureaucratic constriction and the inevitable tendency of public monopolies to hold up prices, you can be thankful that the motor car preceded modern socialist doctrines of state management. Had they existed 150 years ago the coach drivers' union would have been demanding ever bigger subsidies. Many activities, such as the Royal Mail and refuse collection, fare so badly under "public" ownership that farming them out should be considered.

HINDRANCES IN THE MARKET

The market system in Britain has suffered from three tendencies, apart from government intervention, which have undermined its efficiency. First, the worship of size, served by the tax system. "Economies of scale", "bigger means better"—these were the cries of 15 years ago. It suited the bureaucratic attitude in industry to create bigger empires and hope they would become monopolies. It suited the mood of technological determinism which presumed to tell the human race it must go wherever science and technology directed, regardless of morality or utility. It led to the collapse of several famous firms particularly in the motor industry. The taxation system favoured amalgamations. Selling your business was at that time one of making money. Take-over bidders sold off assets. The big firm could feed itself from profits ploughed back.

Second, restrictive practices and inadequate invest-ment. It takes five British workers to equal one Japanese in the motor industry. Bethlehem Steel makes as much steel as the British Steel Corporation with half the number of employees. Such are the effects of our restrictive practices, which, incidentally, are just as bad in the professions (especially among lawyers) as they are in industry. In these conditions and with very high taxation on dividends it is no wonder that investment in enterprise is low—especially when the gigantic British debt offers such yields on government stock. This lack of investment has led to demands that the government should invest. On a big scale it would not only lead to inefficiency—governments invest according to bureau-cratic pressures and organised groups. If government intervention in the market destroyed equity investment, they would have no stars to steer by and we would be left in the jungle, at the mercy of whatever interest collared the Treasury. But, worse than this, it would fatally undermine liberty.

Third, there is a fairly widespread cynicism about the conduct of the higher economic and financial man-agement. The financial institutions have been too obsessed with making money for themselves—often by means which appear doubtfully honest. They seem to play too little part in supplying industry with the sinews it requires.

SOCIAL DEMOCRATS AND THE MIXED ECONOMY:
THE "ULTIMATE DILEMMA"

What proportion of the national income must go to the Government? At present 63 per cent passes through its hands. What is the mixture of the mixed economy? Has "public" control gone far enough? Some of the Labour Party's leaders are on the record as saying that if the Government takes any more of the national income freedom and democracy will be threatened. But they show little sign of calling a halt. British social democrats have been riding along on the back of free enterprise avoiding the ultimate dilemma. The idea that you can have total public ownership of all the means of production, distribution and exchange, as is written into the constitution of the Labour Party, together with democracy is absurd and is admitted by the majority of the Labour Party to be absurd.

In the British Parliament the purpose of taxation is inadequately understood. Today, governments control the supply of money. If they want more money they can print it. They do not have to "buy" it from a third party. Taxation more than ever, therefore, is concerned with removing demand by individuals or firms so that resources may be available for government purposes without rampant inflation. But taxation on the very rich has a negligible effect on demand. Taxation on the poor, apart from being unjust, is often off-set by increases in wages. Taxation is effective, therefore, on a narrow but deserving band of taxpayers. As an instrument of demand management it is becoming increasingly ineffective for its main purpose and damaging to the economy.

Taxation and expenditure are never discussed

together. Nor are alternative expenditures discussed together, nor is there any budget of resources. If Members of Parliament were forced to consider how they paid for things at the moment they voted for them to be done, it would at least alert the public to what was happening.

THE COUNTER-CIVIL SERVICE

Parliaments too will have to equip themselves better for such managerial roles as are properly theirs. The democratic representative today is expected to play a more positive role than his predecessor, but the negative, critical, obstructive role must not be abolished. Apart from a more logical handling of the business before it, the British system demands some form of counter-civil service. The Ombudsman is an embryonic (and somewhat mistaken) attempt at such a service. The counter-civil service must not be in addition to our already over-inflated public service. Its successes must be judged by quite different criteria. It must be lodged not in the bureaucratic but in the democratic side of government. It must be associated with voluntary community development. It must be a counterpoise to the power of bureaucratic government and vested organisations.

Human ecosystems are not as obviously self-righting as those of nature. Man is endlessly and pointlessly destructive. But we have eroded many of the natural forces making for equilibrium. Our means of communication, the press and television, excite violence and triviality. Our education does far too little to inculcate the general interest or teach boys and girls to view society as a whole. Defeatism in the West has been fostered partly by the appetite of the press and television to magnify the blots on our society and ignore the appalling dishonesty, inefficiency and oppression in Britain by the failure of our state educational system to teach any general morality.

PRESCRIPTIONS FOR LIBERAL DEMOCRACY

Liberal democracy demands continual respect and attention. It demands recognition of the organic, changing but continuous growth of the community. It requires recognition of the ultimate value attaching to individuals in the community apart from their roles. It demands the rejection of economic or technical determinism, in favour of a system which studies human relationships and seeks by political skill to promote a satisfactory but varied series of such relationships. If liberal democracy is taken for granted, the devils of dictatorship, apathy and the bureaucratic attitudes will take over our society.

Liberal democracy must learn the age-old lesson: that human beings are power hungry, that too much government becomes tyranny, that centres of power outside government should exist but must be kept within bounds and accept responsibilities wider than the furtherance of their particular empires.

Liberal democracy must reject the notion that the "public" sector should be simply that ground which sectional interests anxious to free themselves from economic change have succeeded in winning. The "mixed economy" should mean that, while some operations are removed from the market, subjected to different tests and motives, all operations which must change and which could benefit from competition are submitted to it.

Liberal democracy has to reform its political institutions. The hand of the governed must be strengthened against the establishment. Political parties no longer do this. Many important issues fall outside or across party policies. Fewer people now have faith in the parties, feel that they can be trusted to represent them or agree with their position on all issues. Government must present the issues in an intelligible form, setting out the resources available against possible "public" tasks. It may have to take an historically large share of gross domestic product but should use it to undertake general improvements, for instance, in the environment, not to bolster up particular industries in trouble.

1984?

We must re-assert the humane potential of the individual —his or her liberties. We must extend again their opportunities for choice. But socialism which was founded on a Christian, unselfish, ethic has now become bureaucratic. The trade unions are as greedy as any capitalist organisation. The managers in the nationalised industries demand much the same rewards as those in private industry. Differentials are now the cry. We used to be told that democratic socialism was about financial equality. That claim now could only arouse laughter. Few things are more hypocritical than trade union leaders demanding higher pensions for the old and higher wages for their members. But while losing faith in its own beliefs modern socialism is destroying belief in a free society.

A void is left in politics which must be filled or we shall accelerate down the slope to the corporate state and beyond that to the dictatorship of 1984. There are many signs that Orwell may be proved right.

Politics and Public Policy

THE MORAL DIMENSION

Nigel Lawson, MP

The Author

NIGEL LAWSON was born in 1932 and educated at Westminster School and Christ Church, Oxford. He has been Member of Parliament for Blaby since 1974; an Opposition spokesman on Treasury and Economic Affairs since 1977, and was an Opposition Whip, 1976-77. He was a member of the Editorial Staff, *Financial Times*, 1956-60; City Editor, *Sunday Telegraph*, 1961-63; Editor, *Spectator*, 1966-70. Contributor to *Sunday Times* and *Evening Standard*, 1970-71, and *The Times*, 1971-72.

Special Assistant to the Prime Minister (Sir Alec Douglas-Home), 1963-64. Special Political Adviser, Conservative Party, 1973-74. Author, with Jock Bruce-Gardyne, of *The Power Game* (1976).

The Moral Dimension

There can by now be no doubt that collectivism has failed. Throughout the nations of the industrialised world, the people are freer and their living standards higher the less far-reaching is the degree of state owner-ship, direction and control of the economy. Yet, throughout the industrialised world, the frontiers of the state, so far from being rolled back, are almost everywhere being further extended.

In Britain that great engine of creeping socialism, once accepted uncritically in all Parties, neo-Keynesian demand management, the doctrine which holds that "public" (government) spending must be increased in times of recession and private spending reduced, by tax increases and/or credit squeezes, in times of boom, has at long last been generally discredited and identified as a generator of instability, inflation and industrial debility. Yet once again, in 1978, we find public spend-ing planned to expand at double the expected rate of growth of the economy as a whole.

SOCIALISM'S APPARENT IMMUNITY TO FAILURE

It is now nine years and two Industry Acts since the merger of the Department of Economic Affairs with the Ministry of Technology and the industrial sections of the Board of Trade first gave Britain in effect a

Department of Industry. Those nine years have been the least successful in our long industrial history. Yet detailed government intervention in industry, ostensibly at least directed towards industrial rather than social ends, and now dignified as an "industrial strategy", continues to flourish like the green bay tree.

All the opinion polls suggest that nationalisation has never been more unpopular, as people become increasingly intolerant of the losses of those state corporations that are obliged to compete in world markets and of the service from those that are not. Yet the National Enterprise Board ensures that state ownership inexorably extends. The people cry out for lower taxes and more choice: yet they are given higher government spending, higher taxes (save when a general election is imminent) and less choice. And so it goes on.

Nor is the failure confined to performance. With the exception of the infantile populist syndicalism of Mr Benn, the British Left is bankrupt of ideas, and all its leading men of ideas have either died or departed. In his last major public pronouncement, in 1975, the late Anthony Crosland—the last remaining non-marxist socialist thinker—sadly concluded[1] that the

> "upsurge of public spending has of course required a tight rein on private spending; and the consequent increase in taxes on ordinary working people has without doubt both disappointed expectations and contributed to inflation . . . In the social services, much of the spending has gone on creating large bureaucracies . . ."

Yet the onward march of the state continues remorselessly.

---

[1] *Social Democracy in Europe,* Fabian Tract 438, Fabian Society, 1975.

What is the explanation of this paradox? What is the secret that enables socialist thinking and practice to survive disillusion and intellectual bankruptcy, and to rise and rise again from the ashes of its own failure? This is the question to which an answer must be found.

We must discover the secret—and its antidote. Those of a more revolutionary disposition may perhaps be content to wait for continuing failure to bring, eventually, its own nemesis, in the hope of being able to build a radically new order out of the rubble of the old. But for those who, while not content with merely slowing the pace of deterioration, nevertheless believe in the overriding virtue of evolutionary change, of piecemeal progress towards a liberal market economy, this option is out. What, then, is the key that will turn the lock?

ETATISM APPEALS TO POLITICIANS/BUREAUCRATS

The first and most obvious explanation of the apparent inevitability of socialism, its apparent immunity to its own failure, might seem to lie in its seductive appeal to the governing classes (and their camp followers). Economic decisions which, in a liberal order, are widely diffused among the people, under socialism fall to be taken by a relatively small number of politicians and bureaucrats. This transfer and concentration of power has obvious attractions to the politicians and bureaucrats themselves—particularly those culturally conditioned to a contempt for trade, commerce and the profit motive. (It is a particularly malign chance that has seen the luxury of late nineteenth century aristocratic snobbism embraced by the bourgeois Left of to-day.)

But while this may be one reason why the open society is unlikely to commend itself to a dictator, it is unconvincing as an explanation of the persistence of socialism in a genuine democracy, as ours is, despite its faults. However strong the appeal of power to the governing classes, the need for electoral support comes first. The onward march towards collectivism can happen only if the people either want it, or at least are afraid to turn back. But in what sense do they want it? Mr Arthur Seldon's excellent book *Charge,* for example, is imbued with a passionate conviction that the ordinary people of Britain desire the very reverse: want *more* freedom, *more* choice, *more* opportunity to spend their own money in their own way, and that it is only the perversity of politicians and the shortcomings of the system that frustrate them. In the first part of his thesis, I am sure he is fundamentally right—and he could well have added that the desire to own private property is one of the deepest and most fundamental instincts of mankind. But I am not convinced of the second part: that the nigger in the woodpile is the politician.

THE STATE AS PORK-BARREL

The plain fact is that half a century of creeping socialism under all Parties has turned the State increasingly into a vast pork-barrel, out of which everyone is anxious to extract at least as much as the next man—and to hang on to it. Put less crudely, creeping socialism has created powerful vested interests among the governed. Put still more politely, the problem is Burke's "prescription".

Perhaps the clearest instance of pork-barrel politics is so-called industrial policy—which in practice invariably turns out to be an *anti*-industrial policy. For complain though it does about various forms of state behaviour, the private sector by and large welcomes its embrace and is all too ready to be corrupted by it.

This is hardly surprising. Not only does the State come bearing promises of government contracts and financial support—and who has ever said "go away" to Santa Claus? It is also prepared to make the difficult choices for industry, to insure it against most of the consequences of failure and, perhaps most attractive of all, to replace the rigours of competition with the comforts of government-blessed co-operation in what is alleged to be the national interest.

Yet another significant example of the vested interest created by the State was recently described by Professor Ralf Dahrendorf[2] as "the educational class":

> ". . . something like 10 per cent of all voters are involved full-time in educational institutions . . . They are all once removed from the wealth-creating parts of society; indeed they are largely children of public expenditure, and their interests are determined by this . . . There is a tendency for members of the educational class to support progressive parties and, if they do not, they are quite likely to dissociate themselves from this class . . . a development I find highly regrettable . . . First, educational class progressiveness usually has little to do with what those who do not belong want . . . Second, a society dominated by the educational class is not likely to be either very liberal or very effective in economic terms."

If this is one vested interest that derives a special importance from the key role of education in modern society, overall it is the sheer numbers that impress. More than one worker in five is directly employed by

[2] *The Times Higher Education Supplement,* 13 July, 1978.

government, central or local. If we add to these all those attending full-time education; all those, like the workers at British Leyland, whose jobs depend on government bounty; all those in private industry—not to mention the public corporations—whose fortunes depend on government contracts; and all those (not simply the pensioners) whose income is largely derived from state benefits; then we almost certainly have *a majority of the adult population substantially dependent on state patronage.*

No wonder, then, if a sizeable and growing section of the people, however genuine its preference for increased choice and lower taxes, is more profoundly moved by the fear of losing what it has. Nor is it any answer to argue that, if the frontiers of the state were rolled back, all would be better off; for each individual is concerned with his own particular vested interest, and any potential threat to it. What guarantee has he that his tax bill will be lower because the State spends less on *him*? What is true in general (that taxpayers as a body will gain) is by no means self-evident in the particular (that any given taxpayer will gain).

EDMUND BURKE AND PRESCRIPTIVE RIGHTS: CONTINUITY OR STATE POWER?

Looking at it another way, what the would-be liberal reformer confronts is Burke's concept of "prescriptive rights"—the claims and practices legitimised by long usage. "When men are encouraged to go into a certain mode of life by the existing laws", he wrote in his *Reflections on the Revolution in France,* "and protected in that mode as in a lawful occupation . . . I am sure it is unjust in legislature, by an arbitrary act, to offer a sudden violence to their minds and feelings."

There is a profound irony here. Instinctively, the liberal conservative follows Burke and respects prescription—and indeed vested interests—as necessary elements of continuity and stability in society. Yet there has now grown up, what Burke could never have envisaged: the prescriptive rights and vested interests of socialism—a creed dedicated to the achievement of a radical change in society. And there is something particularly disquieting when these rights and interests, so far from being bastions against state power, are in practice rights to, and interests in, state bounty and state dependence.

Yet although we are now much closer to understanding the persistence of a socialist order despite its manifest failure in practice, I do not believe we have yet uncovered the real obstacle to the recreation of the open society. The prescriptive rights and vested interests of socialism are indeed barriers to the radical transformation that some liberal thinkers may dream about, but they need not prevent gradual and evolutionary change —as history has amply demonstrated in other contexts. It was in this longer time-scale that Keynes rightly wrote his celebrated concluding sentence of the *General Theory*: "But, soon or late, it is ideas, not vested interests, which are dangerous for good or evil".

TRADE UNION POWER: THE STATE AS COUNTERVAILING POWER

Before identifying the idea which, I believe, lies at the root of the problem, we must consider the role of trade union power. The leadership has been consciously socialist ever since trade unionism spread from skilled

workers to unskilled workers in the wake of the great
dock strike of 1889. Must we conclude that, regardless
of the majority of the people, and indeed of ordinary
trade unionists, the big trade union leaders have an
effective veto on any change that is not towards more
socialism? Is their baronial power such that the rest of
the population in general, and management in particular, are obliged to look to the State to provide the only
possible countervailing power?

Certainly, many would claim this to be the explanation for, and justification of, the battery of state controls
on prices, incomes and profits that constitute as sinister a
threat to the open society as does the ever-growing
share of the nation's resources appropriated by the
State. I must confess it has always seemed to me
perverse to regard the conferring of political power on
trade union leaders, in return for a promise to exercise
less economic power, either as a diminution in their
power or as a good in itself. But real though the problem of trade union power undoubtedly is, and malign
though many of its consequences may be, its role in the
context of the conundrum posed in this essay is, I
believe, far less than is generally imagined.

BAGEHOT AND ROBERT LOWE

After all, there is nothing new about it. More than a
century ago, Bagehot, for example, was much concerned with the power and nature of trade unions and
wrote frequently of the need for legal reform and of the
effects of trade unions on prices and wages. Here he is,
in 1859, inveighing against the closed shop:

"The law is as favourable to associations of working men
as it ought to be, or as in a community such as ours it

could be expected to be. It allows all labourers to form a society for the purpose of raising the price of *their own* labour, and it allows them also by all peaceable means to induce or persuade other persons not to work for less than their price. But trade unions now, and whilst human nature is human nature always will, go further. If not by bodily violence, by continual and latent coercion they endeavour to compel persons who do *not* belong to their society to cease from working."

Again, the best (if somewhat jaundiced) analysis of the political economy of trade unionism I have so far read is to be found in an unsigned article in the *Quarterly Review* of October 1867, written by Gladstone's first Chancellor of the Exchequer, Robert Lowe. His opening sentence sets the tone:

"The question of Trades' Unions, since the Reform Bill has been carried, and perhaps on that very account, is the most momentous to which any writer can address himself."

On the false economics of militant trade unionism:

"We do not find fault with the policy of Trades' Unions for being selfish; what we object to is that, meaning to be selfish, it is actually suicidal."

But the essential problem is political, and to this end Lowe recommends reform of trade union law, concluding with these words:

"The law will then be adequate to the mischief. If it can be enforced, society will have freed itself from a great peril; dangers to our manufactures and commerce, the amount of which no man can measure, will have been arrested, and a demoralisation which threatens to lower the character of the English operative to the level of the

Thug of India will have been stayed; if not, we must be prepared to see our prosperity wither and perish under the ruinous influence of persons as ignorant of their own true interests as they are careless of the feelings and reckless of the interests of others."

In the century and more that has elapsed, trade union power has always been with us. Sometimes it has appeared more acute, sometimes less—the fluctuations depending partly on outside events and partly on the skill with which the government of the day addressed itself to the problem. But intrinsically it is no different now from what it was at the time of Bagehot and Lowe in the mid-nineteenth century—nor, contrary to popular belief, has the trade union movement as such gone very far towards the realisation of their fear: that it would turn its power to the achievement of explicitly political ends. Thus we have to look elsewhere for the explanation of the much more recent and seemingly inevitable erosion of liberal democracy and the open society.

SUPREMACY OF THE MORAL OVER THE ECONOMIC AND POLITICAL

To find the true explanation, the true secret that enables state socialism to survive disillusion, intellectual bankruptcy, and above all its own incontrovertible practical failure, we have to look, with Keynes, to the realm of ideas—but not to ideas in the economic or political sense. It is the moral dimension that lies at the heart of the matter. For man is a moral animal, and no political or economic order can long survive except on a moral base. Socialists have always understood this;

Conservatives and Liberals (and most sensible men are conservative in politics and liberal in economics) have latterly seemed not to do so.

Thus it is that, while the economic battle of ideas has undoubtedly been won, the political battle of ideas has not. For, at the end of the day, politics is about moral issues. Indeed, it might be argued that the only successful piece of nationalisation ever undertaken in this country has been the most important one of all: the nationalisation of morality, which has occurred as duties and obligations are increasingly removed from the personal sphere and assumed by government.

The nationalisation of morality, the arrogation to the public sphere of something that rightly belongs to the private sphere, has in fact done untold harm. We have now reached a stage in which private action—in the economic field, taken in its broadest sense, at least— is automatically considered morally inferior to public or state action. This imbalance can be seen most clearly in people's attitude to profit—the cornerstone of the capitalist economic system. From time to time eminent public figures, from the Chancellor of the Exchequer downwards, protest that no-one any more considers "profit" to be a dirty word. But morality is best illuminated not by generalisations but by specific instances.

To take just one example, many people have been concerned at the rising tide of pornography. A good number are genuinely concerned at what they see as its intrinsically offensive and corrupting character. Many more, if pressed, are found to be most offended because pornography appears to be *profitable*. Indeed, if the pornographers were starving in their garrets, instead of luxuriating in their Bentleys, many of today's objectors would probably be launching a powerful campaign for them to be subsidised by the Arts Council.

Again, most of the numerous letters I received, as a Member of Parliament, objecting to the consequences of the 1967 Abortion Act, were concerned not primarily with the ethical issues: what really aroused the moral conscience of the most articulate section of the nation was the shocked discovery that people were making big money out of these operations.

An example wholly removed from the minefield of sexual morality is the spectacular new crime of the past decade: hijacking and similar forms of so-called urban terrorism. Usually, these evils have been committed in the name of a political cause; yet however intolerable that cause may be, and however evil the act committed in its name, there are always apologists to be found ready to excuse or condone it. If precisely the same criminal act had been committed to extract a wholly non-political ransom payment—for financial rather than "political" gain—it would be the subject of universal execration.

And what is nowadays the most morally laudable epithet that can be applied to any institution, as the ultimate commendation? It is, surely, that the institution in question is a "non-profit-making" body.

NATIONALISATION OF MORALS: MORAL SUPERIORITY OF STATE OVER PRIVATE ACTION

What is the reason for this new morality that exalts public action and deplores private action, and which reserves the strongest moral opprobrium for the profit motive, the lynchpin of the capitalist system upon which the material well-being of the people is based? Three separate strands can be disentangled.

First, there is the depressing belief that life is a zero-sum game; that one man's gain is necessarily another man's loss, and that profit therefore inevitably implies exploitation. If this were true, economic growth would be impossible, and we would never have emerged from our caves.

Second, and still inculcated in our schools, is a perfectly proper revulsion against the condition of the urban poor during the Industrial Revolution. It is proper for a system to be judged by its results; but what has happened is a particularly perverse form of transference. The opprobrium that originally attached to the capitalist system, because of some of its early results, has now been transferred to the system itself—despite the fact that it can now be seen that it produces more material well-being, and less poverty and suffering, than any other system.

Third, perhaps the most important strand in the new morality is the notion that capitalism is based on self-interest, whereas socialism is founded on much higher motives. Certainly, capitalism is based on self-interest (if by that term we include the desire of a man to benefit not merely himself but his family—a vitally important extension with far-reaching implications). But self-interest is not peculiar to the capitalist system: it is the condition of mankind. All of us, business man or bureaucrat, are motivated, not wholly but largely, by self-interest. The only difference is that, while the self-interest of the business man leads directly to the satisfaction of the demands of others, the self-interest of the bureaucrat does not. It is hard, therefore, to discern any moral superiority in the latter. The truth is that the business man, and, in particular, his apologists, from Adam Smith down, are honest about their own motives, whereas the politicians and the bureaucrats are not.

Indeed, were it not that all human beings are motivated largely by self-interest, as defined earlier, it is difficult to see how a free society or indeed any large-scale society could possibly be governable. It is no accident that monastic communities, which exclude self-interest, are typically (a) small and (b) regulated on authoritarian principles.

MORAL SUPERIORITY OF VOLUNTARY CAPITALISM OVER COERCIVE STATE

This distinction, indeed, illumines a most important dimension of morality in which capitalism is clearly superior to socialism. Capitalism is essentially based on voluntarism—the idea of voluntary co-operation and voluntary exchange—whereas socialism, disapproving of the results of voluntarism, is essentially based on coercion, on the use of force by the State.

Nevertheless, we have at last identified the secret of socialism; the fundamental obstacle blocking the path of a return to the open society. The apologists of capitalism have hoped to win the day on the merit of its fruits, and have unwisely allowed the moral dimension to go by default. The apologists of the barren tree of socialism, by contrast, have played the moral card for all it is worth—and a good deal more besides.

If the seemingly inevitable drift towards collectivism and away from the open society is to be reversed, the prime requirement is for those who wish to see this to recognise the importance of the moral dimension, to seize the moral initiative, and to win the moral argument. This should not be difficult—although, after all these years, it will inevitably take time: the problem is that, so far, it has scarcely even been attempted. It should not be difficult, partly for the reasons indicated above, but even more because socialism in practice is not merely devoid of the moral superiority it likes to claim: it is positively and fundamentally immoral based as it is on envy and class hatred.

The envy inherent in socialist egalitarianism has long been noted. As Oliver Wendell Holmes wrote to Harold Laski in 1927:

> "I have no respect for the passion for equality, which seems to me merely idealising envy—I don't disparage envy, but I don't accept it as legitimately my master."

Anthony Crosland, in the first (1956) edition of his important book, *The Future of Socialism*, went so far as to discuss, openly, the necessity for the Labour Party to base its appeal on the envy of the less well off—although in later editions this section was considerably abridged. Even so, in his 1975 Fabian Tract, he was obliged to admit that egalitarian socialism was not primarily concerned with improving the lot of the less well off:

> ". . . the argument for more equality is based not on any direct material gain to the poor, but on the claims of social and natural justice."

Natural justice it cannot be; and the myth of "social justice" has been irreparably demolished by Professor Hayek. As for the exploitation of class hatred, its articulation has usually been left to less eminent expositors of socialism (such as Mr Michael Meacher in his long *New Statesman* article of January 1974, gloatingly entitled "The Coming Class War"), but it is no less central for that.

It may seem incredible that a creed based on those two most destructive of emotions, envy and hatred, should have even aspired to, let alone gained, a moral ascendancy. The explanation is that it has been able to do so by default. For their neglect of the moral dimension of politics (and economics), the champions of the open society have only themselves to blame. Until that neglect is ended, and the moral initiative seized—and time is fast running out—they will continue to find themselves winning the economic battles, and losing the political war.

PART IV

INTELLECTUAL DISSENT AND THE REVERSAL OF TRENDS*

The Duke of Edinburgh

*An edited and shortened version of a broadcast, "Us in 2000", in October 1977 on Radio Clyde, in a series entitled "Platform: Towards 2000". It has been re-titled for this book and sub-headings inserted. We thank the broadcaster and the radio station for permission to use the material here.

Intellectual Dissent and the Reversal of Trends

I

INTRODUCTION: KINDS OF PREDICTION

It is one thing to predict technological developments; it is rather more difficult to predict general social and political conditions. And there is a considerable difference between what is likely to happen and what we may want to happen. I am going to be concerned only with what I think may happen. What I would like to see happen is an entirely different story.

(i) OBJECTIVE ANALYSIS OF CAUSES: 1984

The objective approach to forecasting entails trying to comprehend the principal factors which have influenced the broad sweep of political and social history and then to continue the process on a speculative basis into the future. One could study the political, social, economic and moral circumstances which have led to the establishment of dictatorships and then try to identify any common denominators. One could then look at our own situation today, for instance, to see if any of those denominators are present and to make a forecast accordingly. The classic example is George Orwell's *1984*.

(ii) EXTRAPOLATION OF TRENDS: CLUB OF ROME

Another alternative for the forecaster is to bring scientific techniques to his aid. He can use a process of statistical extrapolation. He can work out trends from historic figures and then simply extend the trends. This technique has been made much easier by computers. Indeed, the Club of Rome stirred up quite a to-do when it published *The Limits to Growth*,[1] based on this type of computer-aided analysis and prediction.

One of the factors it analysed is the world's population statistics. Because the historical and present figures are reasonably well known, computers can be used to produce trends and predictions for as far ahead as anyone likes. And you do not have to look very far ahead to get a nasty shock. The computers tell us that the world's population will have doubled by the end of the century—only 22 years from now. However, even the relatively simple business of predicting population sizes is not always accurate. Almost every postwar prediction about the growth and structure of our own population has been wrong. One of the consequences has been the recent rather sudden run-down of teacher training colleges.

Computer-assisted prediction has attractions, but it is not without its flaws, as the critics of *The Limits to Growth* were quick to point out. It is obviously impossible to take every eventuality into account or to predict the unpredictable, and in any case you cannot feed values into a machine. Even an intelligent guess at

[1] [Donella H. Meadows, Dennis L. Meadows, Jorgen Randers and William W. Behrens, Potomac Associates, 1972 (Pan Books, London, 1974).–ED.]

the consequences of a disaster, such as a nuclear war or the explosion of a super nova in our galaxy, could be wildly inaccurate; and the future of the world's supplies of energy is not predictable with much accuracy either.

Furthermore, it does not admit the possibility of negative feedback. It is not possible to estimate accurately at what point sheer lack of food will begin to limit the rate of increase in population. Nor is there any way of knowing whether, and to what extent, deliberate attempts to limit population growth will have an appreciable effect. We know that, as the world's population increases, so does the total number of poor and under-nourished. The irony is that increased food production and distribution, and improved technology in the developing countries, tend to encourage increases in population.

You can raise the same sort of objections to the predictions based on statistical extrapolation, although even the most severe critics would acknowledge that, while they are not positively accurate, they are patently not entirely false. The world's population may not exactly double in the next 22 years, but it is certainly going to get very much bigger, virtually whatever happens.

II

THE FALLIBILITY OF THE FORECASTERS

DANGER OF WISHFUL THINKING . . .

Quite apart from the techniques of forecasting, there is the attitude of the forecaster to bear in mind. I suppose it may be humanly possible to be utterly objective, but I rather doubt it. If you have grown up with or acquired a certain set of principles, they will inevitably colour your selection of historical factors and the emphasis you give to the conclusions you draw from them. In any event there is such a vast choice of material that the less scrupulous prophets find it easier to start with the conclusion they wish to reach and then simply search around for the appropriate cases to prove it. I cannot avoid selecting the historical factors, but I hope I have not fallen into the trap of pre-selecting my conclusions.

Pre-selection is really nothing better than wishful thinking, but it is particularly popular with political salesmen. Many people have imagined a state of Utopia where everything is ideal. Having presupposed that it is practically and humanly possible to achieve such a state, it only remains for them to devise a means of reaching it. Once the first moves are made along this primrose path, the consequences are never exactly what was originally envisaged. Indeed, I think it could be shown that Utopian legislation almost always has exactly the opposite effect to what was originally intended.

Consequently, Utopia remains as far away as ever and the community finds itself landed with a whole crop of new and unexpected problems. It is one of the characteristics of Utopia salesmen that they are convinced that their doubtless laudable ends justify whatever means they choose to employ. They can only assume that organised violence and terror are a means to a better end but, unfortunately, the community has to suffer the means while the Utopian end is never likely to be achieved.

. . . AND LACK OF REALITY

Devotion to an idea to such an extent that it blinds one to reality is the equal and opposite danger to the refusal to recognise reality because it may be unpleasant. In the first case, the most frightful horrors are condoned because they are justified by the greatness of the idea. Such are the Inquisition, revolutionary terrorism and the Gulag Archipelago. In the second case, the most appalling conditions are allowed to continue because it is so easy to ignore them. Such were slavery, abject poverty and slum housing.

The trouble is that reality is like a lettuce: you have to peel off a lot of leaves before you get to its heart. But you must get to reality, or to the nearest possible approximation to it, if you are going to have any chance at all of looking into the future. The computer analysis is a good example. If, for whatever reason, you feed the wrong factors into a computer, or if you give them the wrong emphasis, or if you leave out vital factors, the machine will still give you an answer, but completely misleading.

PRACTICAL DIFFICULTIES IN PREDICTION

There are also two purely practical problems about predicting what life might be like in these islands in the year 2000.

INTELLECTUAL FASHION: AT HOME . . .

First, every so often popular attention seems to become focussed on some entirely novel and unexpected consideration, and this naturally tends to confuse earlier predictions. Some years ago the issues of starvation, malnutrition and world population gave rise to the Freedom from Hunger Campaign. This was followed by a sudden concern for the conservation of nature and the environment. More recently, interest switched to energy resources and alternative sources of energy. Each has had quite a significant influence on popular attitudes. Who knows what will be next to attract public attention? Perhaps it will be the problems of a changing world climate, or it may be a revival of interest in religion. Whatever it is, it is bound to make predictions based on current attitudes turn out to be less accurate, if not completely wrong.

. . . AND ABROAD

Secondly, we cannot exist totally isolated from the rest of the world. There is no way of knowing what ideas and attitudes will sweep into this country from abroad, or what political or practical events will have repercussions here. The waves of international subversion and terrorism are already lapping our shores and may have all sorts of unpredictable consequences.

III

FACTORS IN FORECASTING

One of the most important factors we should take into account before trying to look into the future is ordinary human nature. If we are going to consider the future in these islands, we should examine it as it appears in the British character.

(i) PRIMACY OF HUMAN NATURE

We know certain fundamentals. Most people react to circumstances from the point of view of their own self-interest. A farmer's reaction to higher food prices is obviously going to be different from that of the house-wife. That very observant and down to earth 18th-century economist, Adam Smith, put it in a nutshell:

> "It is not from the benevolence of the butcher, the brewer or the baker that we expect our dinner, but from their regard to their own interests . . ."

Attitudes in general tend to be coloured by the point from which a view is taken. Take the discussion about the economy and unemployment. Governments and academic economists tend to be concerned with the figures of unemployment and official job-creation schemes. Employers are concerned with wealth-creation for the benefit of those involved: investors, managers and the workforce. Consequently, govern-ments see investment in new industrial plants as a way of increasing employment, whereas employers see its value in the prospect of increasing productivity or out-put, and giving a reasonable return on the investment. Trade unions, on the other hand, are inclined to see automation and increase in productivity naturally as a threat to existing jobs. From yet a different point of view, more efficient production could be said to release relatively unproductive workers for more promising employment in new enterprises.

But these are all group reactions. Each individual has his own attitude depending on the situation in which he finds himself and the sort of person he is.

(ii) UBIQUITY OF SELF-INTEREST: ETHICALLY NEUTRAL

Self-interest is certainly the most powerful character-istic in most people, and it does not only apply in the strictly economic sense. Politicians, bureaucrats, social snobs and even churchmen have a primary interest in the activity that occupies their attention. Like all the facets of life, ambition and self-interest are neither good nor bad in themselves. They become good or bad only in the way individuals give them expression.

The unscrupulous pursuit of ambition and self-interest without restraint, whether by individuals or groups, for whatever purpose, has always ended in disaster.

In practice the freedom to pursue self-interest, whether by individuals or groups, has always been ac-companied by some form of restraint. The oldest and crudest is simply fear of retaliation or revolution, but this leads to conflict and eventually to a balance of weakness. Then there is the law, but that is only as good as the legislators make it, as sensible as the judges inter-pret it, as effective as its enforcement. The only com-pletely certain restraint is self-control based on the voluntary acceptance of certain moral and ethical standards and principles.

(iii) SELF-IMPOSED LAW

This has been a country in which individuals have been inspired by or, to put it another way, have had their behaviour modified by the "Christian ethic". If there is one thing which can be predicted with any certainty, it is that if we abandon the Christian doctrine of loving our neighbour and the personal responsibility of each individual for his actions, we shall most certainly revert to a state of jungle warfare. Expediency will be the only criterion for decisions.

A distinguished English judge, speaking 50 years ago, put it this way:

"to my mind the real greatness of a nation, its true civilisation, is measured by the extent of this law of obedience to the unenforceable. It measures the extent to which a nation trusts its citizens, and its existence and area testify to the way they behave in response to that trust. Mere obedience to law does not measure the greatness of a nation . . . The true test is the extent to which individuals can be trusted to obey self-imposed law".

Therefore any remotely objective estimate of what life is going to be like, as opposed to mere prophecies of doom, depends to a very large extent on an assessment of the ethical, moral and spiritual values which people are likely to adopt.

(iv) MORAL PRINCIPLES AND PUBLIC ATTITUDES

History shows that, without a deep moral conviction, how easy it is for practical circumstances and human attitudes to react with each other to produce wholly irrational and unpredictable situations. It was the combination of the doctrines of Hitler's National Socialist German Workers' Party—more commonly known as Nazi—with a latent popular prejudice against Jews, which produced the concentration camps and gas chambers. This ghastly inhumanity was certainly not in keeping with the normal behaviour of the German people and quite beyond the range of expectation. But it is a latent danger in every country.

So any assessment of the future depends on an estimate of which way the battle for minds is going to go; by which ethical, moral and spiritual principles personal and public attitudes are going to be influenced. For it seems to me that the criterion for a civilised society is not its technological standards nor even its material prosperity; it is the degree of humanity and sense of well-being among its people. The factor which governs this well-being is not more and more legislation—but the understanding of and commitment to unenforceable law.

IV

HUMAN RIGHTS OR STATE PRIVILEGES

This raises a fundamental issue of principle on which the whole nature of a civilisation depends. Are there any such things as inherent human rights, or is all power vested in the state whose officials concede privileges to individual citizens? If the state is all-powerful, who is to see that its powers are not abused? Furthermore, who is to decide what constitutes an abuse in the first place?

The glib answer is that in a democracy the people decide, but can the people decide absolutely everything? If so, what happens to individual human rights?

The alternatives are starkly clear. Reduced to extremes, the choice is between a philosophy which holds that all individual citizens must serve the general public interest, which means, in effect, that the individual becomes a servant of the state, or, alternatively, a philosophy which asserts that the individual is of paramount importance and that therefore the state exists to preserve and protect his human rights to liberty and integrity. But if we accept that the individual is of paramount importance, we must also accept that individuals, whatever their job or occupation, must have a common moral code to guide their attitudes and actions. Without this essential qualification a free society would be reduced to anarchy.

This is not a new choice. Every generation in every community has to make this decision at some time or another. The obvious choice would be in favour of the philosophy of the individual. Unfortunately, such a system depends upon individual restraint and good sense, and it is really too much to expect that everybody will behave like an angel all the time. It is this human weakness which is always seized upon by the zealous reformers and those who always know better, to justify their ambition to order the lives of their fellow citizens.

CHOICE IN THE POLITICAL MARKET

Whichever choice is adopted or imposed it is always easy to find fault with it. But, provided there is open competition to find fault and to offer remedies, all is reasonably well. However, this freedom of choice in the political market can only be maintained by individuals who see its value as a guarantee of their personal freedom and who make their judgement of political programmes against a clear understanding of the likely consequences. If the choice is made simply on the basis of what looks most attractive and expedient at the time,

or from a short-sighted view of self-interest, the consequences are usually disastrous.

CONTROLS AND BUREAUCRACY SHIFT POWER

Corrections of real or imagined faults lead to controls;
controls lead to more faults and even more control.
Then, as the controls mount up, the costs and the
bureaucracy required to operate them begin to escalate
and the emphasis is no longer on the welfare of the
individuals but on the economic viability of the State.
Gradually—and always with the very best intentions
and almost unnoticed by the people—the power of
decision passes from the individual to a ruling group.
And the more power a ruling group gathers to itself the
more it seeks to protect its position against individual
opposition and criticism.

Once the law ceases to protect the rights of the individual from the gang—any gang—freedom is lost.
There is a large and growing number of countries which
have got into this situation, and there is ample evidence
of the restrictive way of life which has developed within
them, even to the extent of forcibly preventing their
citizens from leaving the country if they should try to do
so.

In the event the choice is never presented to people
in such simple terms because, even though freedom is
indivisible, each individual only sees it from his point
of view. The media will fight if the freedom of the press
is threatened; the law will fight for its independence;
the business man will fight for his right to exercise his
initiative; the worker will struggle for his right to join
or not to join a union; and so on; but few of them

recognise that an attack on the liberty of any one of them is an attack on the liberty of all of them. Once a determined government begins the process of eroding human rights and liberties—always with the best possible intentions—it is very difficult for individuals or for individual groups to stand against it.

INDIVIDUALS OR GROUPS

On freedom of expression, George Orwell said:

"The big public do not care about the matter one way or the other. They are not in favour of persecuting the heretic and they will not exert themselves to defend him. They are at once too sane and too stupid to acquire the totalitarian outlook."

He would probably have agreed that the big public is neither sufficiently interested nor sufficiently knowledgeable to be able to foresee the likely consequences of certain policies in the face of endlessly repeated assurances that they are for its own ultimate benefit.

If the choice is to be made in favour of the State remaining the servant of the individual, a very large proportion of the population, including those with political ambitions, must make a definite commitment to that choice as a matter of principle.

It means, amongst other things, that the national interest must include the interests of the individual and not be limited to the self-interest of the ruling group or any other organisation exercising power on behalf of a sectional interest. It means that economic policies must include the welfare of individual enterprises and not be based entirely on a statistical analysis and national averages. Above all, it means taking a realistic view of human nature—with all its faults and with all its virtues—and trusting the majority of individuals to pursue their own interests to the benefit of their fellow citizens and consequently to the benefit of the State as a whole.

REVERSING THE TREND

Extrapolation from the recent past suggests that the State, which means in practice its professional administrators and political party officials, will have achieved almost complete responsibility by the end of the century. On the other hand, a backward look at the broad sweep of history suggests that the people of this country allow certain trends to go so far and then almost at the last moment begin to appeciate where they are being led and, by an obstinate refusal to co-operate, the trend is gradually reversed. This has happened in a number of periods of British history.

DISSENTING INTELLECTUALS: A NEW TREND?

History suggests that the reversal of trends usually begins with dissenting intellectuals. The present trend towards the nebulous concept of social justice began in the universities some 40 years ago in the depression of the 1930s. It was the liberal-intellectual dissent, combined with other factors, that led to the Russian revolution, which today is itself being criticised by a new generation of liberal-intellectual dissidents. It should come as no surprise to find that the majority of the current crop of international terrorists come from prosperous, liberal-minded, middle-class families.

In this country, there are a number of centres of dissent from the conventional economic policies of the post-war years. Whether the dissenters are right or wrong and whether this represents the beginning of a new trend I would not like to say. What is more important is that, for those people who are prepared to take an interest, the alternatives are there, and, of course, the future direction of events will depend on the choices we make during the next few years.

The argument is not about intentions. All suggestions for political and social reforms are made with the ultimate intention of making life more tolerable and satisfying for the greatest number of people. "The greatest good for the greatest number." Political argument is seldom about ends, it is about the means required to achieve them. All the political catchwords like liberty, equality, fraternity, social justice and human rights can be applied to justify almost any theory or programme intended to benefit the people. Unfortunately, good intentions do not justify the failure in practice of particular theories and programmes.

DEMOCRACY: RULE OF MAJORITY?

We have developed a theory of democracy which holds that the will of the majority shall always prevail. This is very different from the concept of democracy as a system for arriving at a consensus of opinion and of finding a compromise between conflicting points of view: where simple head counting is only used for special purposes.

Quite important consequences flow from the new theory of democracy. In an industrialised country, the proportion of people living in cities and working in the major industries is much larger than those living in small towns and villages and working in small companies or on the land. Furthermore, the proportion of un-skilled workers in industry is much larger than the total of skilled, managerial, self-employed and professional people combined. And a new factor which will become increasingly significant is that the people employed directly and indirectly by local and central govern-ment may soon outnumber all other groups put to-gether.

Applying the rule of self-interest in human nature, it is not very difficult to estimate the trend of decisions in a modern democratic state. But legislative decisions can be thwarted by minorities. The early trade unions demonstrated very effectively how determined action by groups, united by genuine grievances, could impose their will on a hostile majority. While this sort of action can be justified in exceptional cases, it might create new problems if it led to a sort of gang warfare between different minority interest groups.

V

PREDICTIONS

REDUCED CHOICE

It looks as if we can expect to see an increasing bureau-cratic involvement in virtually every aspect of the lives of individual citizens. If the experience of other countries is anything to go by, this will mean a gradual reduction in the freedom of choice and individual re-sponsibility, particularly in such things as housing, the education of children, health care, the ability to acquire or inherit personal property, to hand on commercial enterprises, and the ability to provide for old age through personal savings and, perhaps most important of all, the freedom of the individual to exploit his skills or talents as suits him best.

Judging from the experience of other countries, individual initiative in commerce and industry will become considerably restricted, although the opportunities for marginally legal and illegal activities will increase as a consequence of the growing volume of legislation which it will not be possible to enforce. The situation will also be aggravated if there is any further decline in moral standards and what the judge described as "self-imposed law".

MORE BLACK MARKETS

The major financial and commercial markets will decline, but black markets will begin to flourish. Consumer products will tend towards an average standard, with the gradual elimination of items of better quality. The social services, particularly the Health Service, will suffer as government finds it progressively more difficult to meet the rising costs and as it comes up against the rule that the bigger the organisation the more difficult it is to manage.

LESS TAKE-HOME PAY, MORE JOB DISCIPLINE

The take-home element of wages and salaries will become relatively less important as all the major necessities will be provided "free"—in other words, out of taxation—and also because fringe benefits associated with employment and trade unions will increase. This dependence on fringe benefits for even the basic elements of existence will ensure a very high degree of job discipline. The loss of a job will not be cushioned by the accumulation of savings or property. Employment direction may make unemployment benefits more difficult to obtain. Slavery is no more than a system of directed labour and fringe benefits.

MORE NATIONALISM—LESS FREEDOM

Whereas individuals recognise an affinity with individuals in similar occupations in other countries, the existence of an exclusive nation is the vested interest of national governments. The more powerful governments become, the more they tend to encourage a spirit of exclusive nationalism and a hatred and suspicion of anything foreign or multi-national. Official nationalism will lead to increasing state responsibility for cultural, sporting and economic activities and the gradual suppression of anything which does not suit national economic policies or which does not appear to do justice to the national cultural ideal.

UNTHINKABLE?

These predictions sound almost fanciful in the British context. Some of the things I have said may seem unthinkable in this country with its tradition of freedom and tolerance. There were people in many other countries who felt the same way, but the unthinkable happened to them. The Russian dissident Alexander Solzhenitsyn said:

"It is not how the Soviet Union will find a way out of totalitarianism, but how the West will be able to avoid the same fate."

Epilogue

CAN CONFRONTATION BE AVOIDED?

Ralph Harris

The Author

RALPH HARRIS was born in 1924 and educated at Tottenham Grammar School and Queens' College, Cambridge. He was Lecturer in Political Economy at St. Andrews University, 1949-56, and has been General Director of the Institute of Economic Affairs since 1957. He wrote (with Arthur Seldon) *Hire Purchase in a Free Society, Advertising in a Free Society, Choice in Welfare,* etc., for the IEA. His essay, 'In Place of Incomes Policy", was published in *Catch '76 . . .?* (Occasional Paper "Special" (No. 47), 1976). His most recent works, written with Arthur Seldon, are *Pricing or Taxing?* (Hobart Paper No. 71, 1976) and *Not from Benevolence . . .* (Hobart Paperback No. 10, 1977). He is Secretary of the Wincott Foundation and the Political Economy Club, formerly secretary, now a Vice-President, of the Mont Pelerin Society, and a Council Member of the University College at Buckingham. Mr Harris lectures and writes widely on post-war policies and the economic requirements of a free society.

Can Confrontation be Avoided?

The authors of this symposium reflect many facets of the concern that is increasingly widely felt about the direction in which democratic-corporatist politics seem to be carrying us. Anxiety about the simultaneous erosion of personal freedom, social cohesion and economic progress is shared by thoughtful members of all democratic parties. It is naturally expressed most vehemently by intellectuals who have renounced their early socialist allegiance, such as Patrick Hutber, Paul Johnson, Peter Jay, Woodrow Wyatt, Lord George-Brown, Reg Prentice and veteran J. B. Priestley. But the root cause of concern has been the cumulative failure by both Labour and Conservative administrations to fulfil their repeated promises of a lasting reversal of Britain's decline. Their sorry record has made public men appear inadequate to the challenge of events and led some outside the parties to pin their waning hopes on the emergence of stronger leaders. Yet even if that road was not beset by different dangers for democracy, must we despair of our present men (and women)?

MEASURES NOT MEN . . .

It is by no means clear that post-war cabinets have been led by politicians inferior in character, intellectual endowment or public spirit to those 19th-century "giants" as seen through the telescope of historians. No doubt we all have our favourites and *bêtes-noires* among the assorted Prime Ministers and Chancellors of the Exchequer who have shaped—and mis-shaped—our destinies since 1945: Attlee, Cripps, Churchill, Butler, Macmillan, Selwyn Lloyd, Home, Maudling, Wilson, Jenkins, Heath, Barber, Callaghan, Healey; and we might add, prospectively, Thatcher, Joseph, Howe. Are we so sure that their Victorian predecessors during Britain's heyday were invariably more gifted? The logic of my argument will be that to earn their laurels they did not need to be.

On the hustings it is perhaps inevitable that the more conspicuous failures of the governing party are denounced by the other side as due to personal incompetence or ill-intent. But the speed with which each new administration has been borne down towards collapse—most dramatically since 1964—suggests that the fault was less with the quality of the men than with the collectivist consensus of their measures. Whatever the stature of recent politicians, it can hardly be disputed that even the ablest have been dwarfed by the towering tasks they have tried to discharge. The central question social democrats have always shrunk from confronting is whether the progressive extension of government control—over industry, investment, employment, social welfare, prices, profits, rents and other earnings—could ever be made to work. The sober answer must be that, even if supermen were available to master such a range of issues, they could put the experiment to the test only by arming themselves with even more coercive powers to impose their will over "the economy", which means over all individuals as consumers, workers, entrepreneurs and investors.

When contemporary politicians are moved to admit their failure (usually in private), they will excuse themselves on the ground that the complexity of an advanced economy presents exceptionally difficult problems. This alibi begs the reply that such an economy is therefore all the less amenable to increasingly comprehensive control. Would the reputations of Pitt, Huskisson, Peel, Cobden, Bright, Gladstone have survived if they had set themselves to resist or over-rule market forces in the transformation of cottage industry and canals by the development of textiles, iron and steel, railways and shipbuilding?

THE LIFE-FORCE OF FREEDOM

Despite today's platform rhetoric about "over-mighty Ministers", a paradox of our collectivist age is that the more widely politicians have sought to assert their authority over the market-place the more impotent they are seen to be. The correct response is not simply to attack the "excessive" authority of government, but to limit the range of purposes for which the necessary authority of government is applied.

There is much misunderstanding, not always innocent, of the classical conception of *laissez-faire*. It may therefore require emphasis that the theory and practice of liberal market economy always envisaged an indispensable role for government. The realistic founders of the classical tradition certainly relied for economic progress on the motive force of individual effort, initiative and ambition. This life-force of a dynamic economy and free society, though often scorned by uncomprehending critics as narrow self-seeking, is after all the source of most high achievement. It accounts for the urge to win victory (and prize money) in sport, to earn acclaim (and promotion) in academia, to gain fame (and honours) in philanthropy, or even to achieve high office (and its perquisites) in politics. But the liberal philosophers understood that in the absence of necessary restraints this potent human drive could lead to the enrichment of powerful sectional interests through exploitation of monopoly powers.

It was against such dangers that market economists have embraced competition as a bulwark. So long as alternative suppliers are available, producer "self-seeking" can be served only by serving the sovereign consumer. The best defence of the consumer against a predatory producer is the existence of all other producers. But to ensure the remedy of competition—against the potentially powerful interest of producers in monopoly—requires government to enforce a special kind of legal framework. In essence, it needs legislation to define the respective rights of property-owners, workers, consumers; to enforce contracts and minimum standards of quality, purity, safety; to prohibit restraints on new products or producers. The agenda for government is thus to purge competitive markets of all forms of force and fraud whilst maintaining strong personal incentives for the life-force of high enterprise and exertion.

The resulting market order can be shown to function as a spontaneous *co-operative* endeavour. It permits a division of labour in which individuals pursue their own purposes in fruitful competition with others and exchange the proceeds of their efforts for the goods and services they choose in the market. In this way buyers and sellers reap mutual gains from trade. The guidance mechanism is the network of price signals (including changing rates of wages, profits, rents and interest) which register and transmit information on the shifting pressures of demand and supply. There is a wealth of scholarly literature, extending from Adam Smith to Hayek, Friedman, Robbins, Jewkes, and many younger men, on which IEA authors have drawn since 1957, to show how competitive markets not only harmonise potentially conflicting interests, but economise the use of scarce human and material resources in satisfying the general interest of consumers in abundance, cheapness and choice.

RETREAT TO COLLECTIVISM

The restless search for progress and perfection was bound to call in question the merits of this conception of limited government. Its incomparable success in spreading prosperity and freedom in 19th-century Britain was too easily taken for granted as critics directed attention to blemishes, both real and imaginary.[1]

New methods of production benefited the consumer but threatened existing producer interests (both capital and labour) which naturally demanded protection against "unfair" competition. Theoretical economists began arguing that markets do not in practice conform to the textbook model of "perfect competition". Abstract philosophers agonised over the conflict between the material attainments of the free economy and its supposed indifference to morality. Lofty church-

[1] *The Long Debate on Poverty,* Readings 9, 2nd Edition, IEA, 1974.

men and spiritual sociologists went further in looking for some kind of heaven on earth in which the life-force of individual striving was replaced by the spirit of universal love. And, with the spread of the franchise, competing politicians came increasingly to see short-term electoral advantage in promising to redress every grievance more promptly or more generously than their rivals.

Although dressed up as a benevolent pursuit of the "public interest", political "remedies" took the form of conferring on special interest-groups protection—even immunity—from the general discipline of competition. Whatever the justification of particular reforms, their extension has resulted in the generalisation of monopoly privilege to the point where the earlier presumption in favour of competition no longer offers even token resistance to the most self-serving claims for special treatment. With all the Fabian "inevitability of gradual-ness", what started a century ago as a well-intentioned effort to tame the animal spirits of competitive enter-prise has, by 1978, gone far to subdue its creative drive.

It is not surprising that the increase in production of marketable output is faltering, despite the fertility of modern machinery, while the increase in demand for government favours shows no sign of abating. As political concessions are extended from "special case" to "special case", the anticipated gains are cancelled out and the frustrated beneficiaries soon come back for more.

BIGGER GOVERNMENT NOT BETTER

The spread of disillusion with democratic politics can now be seen to have been inevitable. It is no more than an awakening from the illusion that governments could approach closer to perfection than unavoidably imperfect markets. The besetting sin of politicians can be summed up in words very close to the general confession of the Anglican prayer book: they have done those things which they ought not to have done; and they have left undone those things which they ought to have done. Thus, as Ministers and their multiplying bureaucracies have sought to extend their authority over the marketplace, they have failed to discharge their essential functions on which the stability of the economy and the security of society depend. The collectivist state is like a political conglomerate untrammelled by competition. It is forever diversifying its range of services and policies to the neglect of such primary duties as national defence, the enforcement of law, the upholding of order, the maintenance of competition, the preservation of the value of money, and the discriminating protection of the weak without smothering the strongest impulses towards economic progress.

This failure is sufficiently predictable to warrant a law of political economy which might be entitled the law of increasing marginal futility in policy, comparable to the textbook law of diminishing returns in production. Its brief formulation is that the more widely government enlarges the scale and variety of its activities, the more rapidly its average effectiveness declines. The commonsense explanation is the finite time and talents of even the ablest politicians and the relative scarcity of top executives and administrative abilities available to enforce the multiplying laws. It follows that efficiency will be attenuated as government extends the periphery of policy—what might be called the margin of political cultivation.

MARSHALL ON "CHIVALRY"

This kind of analysis points to the unresolved conflict between economic collectivism and political democracy. Thus the further government seeks to impose its version of the collective interest against the individual's perception of his own and his family's interest, the more political coercion replaces peaceful competition and the heavier the strain it puts on the tolerance and co-operation necessary alike for effective economic performance and social cohesion.

This dilemma was already discernible seventy years ago to Alfred Marshall who, significantly, was led from mathematics to study economics by a "desire to know what was practicable in social reform by State and other agencies". In a powerful essay on the possibility of supplanting self-interest by the more elevated motivation which he called "economic chivalry",[2] he did not scorn the possibility that human nature might become so transformed that "some other civilisation than that which we can now conceive may take the place of that which now exists". Twenty years earlier, in his inaugural lecture[3] at Cambridge, Marshall had called on his students not to leave it to

> "impetuous socialists and ignorant orators to cry aloud that none sought to be shut out by want of material means from the opportunity of leading a life that is worthy of man".

[2] "Social Possibilities of Economic Chivalry" (1907), in A. C. Pigou (ed.), *Memorials of Alfred Marshall*, Macmillan, 1925.

[3] "The Present Position of Economics" (1885), in *Memorials . . ., ibid.*

But he warned against reformers who "in their desire to improve the distribution, are reckless as to the effects of their schemes on the production of wealth". He saw scope for reforms to improve amenities and relieve "those who are weak and ailing through no fault of their own", but he emphasised the proviso that such changes must be made "so as not considerably to slacken the springs of productive energy". Hence his balanced judgement which stands as an indictment of much Liberal, Labour and Conservative policy since he wrote in 1907:

> "The world under free enterprise will fall far short of the finest ideals until economic chivalry is developed. But until it is developed, every step in the direction of collectivism is a grave menace to the maintenance even of our present moderate rate of progress."

MUDDLED MOTIVES FOR MIXED ECONOMY

It is not necessary to go as far as Marshall in conceiving economics as "a science of human motives" in order to glimpse in these passages the root cause of Britain's mounting economic and political disorder. The collapse of post-war hopes for salvation through government planning, nationalisation, state welfare, taxation, subsidisation, regional policy, foreign aid, price and income controls is no doubt the product of many delusions. One myth that has been exploded by experience was that economic requirements and possibilities could be foreseen and guided by politicians and their expert advisers. But the most persistent, deep-seated and crippling source of error that has yet to be eradicated is the presumption that well-intentioned political intervention could easily improve on the imperfect operation of the market economy.

This political conceit rests on an appealing but doubly unfounded dichotomy between "public" and "private" motivation. In the first place, it is a vulgar error to claim superiority for political man pursuing the public interest over economic man pursuing private self-interest. The strength of the case for a free society is based on the truism that all men—whether in markets, politics or even monasteries—are moved to maximum exertion by the widest choice of purposes for which they will apply their varying talents. The propelling power of the aims for which we all strive is not that they are selfish, but that they are *self-chosen* because based on unique personal knowledge. Candid introspection will confirm everyday observation that human action is animated by a mixture of motives and subjective satisfactions which are not easily disentangled, let alone evaluated on a simple scale ranging from good to bad.

But even if "compassionate" politicians could be taken at their own conceit as selflessly pursuing their vision of "the public interest", we are, all the more, driven to ask why they have so consistently failed to achieve their declared aims. At once we encounter the second fallacy, that of confusing motives with results. An intelligent choice between alternative policies does not turn on a subjective judgement of their professed motives but on an objective assessment of their practical outcomes. The most vivid proof of this distinction is seen in housing policy where well-intentioned restrictions on market rents in the (electorally popular) cause of providing "homes for the people" has had precisely the opposite effect of reducing the quantity and quality of rented houses and flats. More generally, this contrast between motives and outcomes in Britain's progressively mixed economy is illuminated by the relative decline in medical care, education, police, libraries, railways, postal, refuse and other services run "in the public interest", compared to the advances in food, clothing, labour-saving domestic equipment, motoring, leisure facilities, colour photography, hi-fi, pocket calculators, yachts, garden furniture, credit facilities and all the other boons produced in response to the "private profit motive".

The explanation made plain by market analysis is that, however self-seeking the motives of private suppliers, competition from alternatives at home or abroad compels them to serve the consumer. This is precisely what Adam Smith meant by the metaphor of an "invisible hand" that led people pursuing their own interests to advance the interests of others. On the other hand, however well-intentioned the motives of Ministers, they have a monopoly in supplying "free" or heavily subsidised services which their involuntary customers have no choice but to pay for through taxation. The key distinction is between freedom in the economic market which peacefully reconciles differing interests and coercion in the political arena which does violence to the interests of minorities and even of majorities.

The economic issue between competitive markets and government monopoly is not a matter of ideological inclination but of scientific analysis. The general superiority of the free market is an inference from the natural universe: it arises from the way the world works, rather than the way critics may think it ought to work. The prime mover of individual, self-chosen purposes is like a tidal force that may, for a time, be dammed but only at mounting cost and with increasing risk of collapse. To the classical insight that the invisible hand of competition operates in the direction of transmuting private interests into public benefits, we can add that the visible fist of political coercion tends to operate contrarily to transform the best intentions into public burdens whose costs are resented and increasingly resisted by tax avoidance, evasion and, not least, emigration.

RULING IDEAS . . .

In the final paragraph of *The General Theory* (1936) Keynes asked whether the fundamental change in policies he recommended was more than "a visionary hope". His magisterial reply is now more often quoted by his critics:

> ". . . the ideas of economists and political philosophers, both when they are right and when they are wrong, are more powerful than is commonly understood. Indeed the world is ruled by little else . . . the power of vested interests is vastly exaggerated compared with the gradual encroachment of ideas. Not, indeed, immediately, but after a certain interval . . ."

It was this belief that inspired the founders of the Institute of Economic Affairs 21 years later in 1957 to question the ruling Keynesian-collectivist consensus in favour of central planning, budgetary fine-tuning, indiscriminate state welfare and the subordination of competitive enterprise to the presumed public interest. A further 21 years on, by 1978, government intervention had grown unevenly, but remorselessly: as measured by public spending, from around 40 per cent to 60 per cent of national income, and by direct public employment from 23 per cent to approaching 30 per cent of the labour force. Does this prove that ideas have lost their potency, or must we allow more time for their gradual encroachment upon policy?

There can be no doubt that recent years have witnessed a dramatic shift of intellectual opinion towards a more limited role for government intervention in the economy. The political conceit about the superior motives and abilities of Ministers and their multiplying bureaucracies has not stood up well to the counter-revolution of market and monetary analysis. What might be called the Hungarian-Cambridge-Harvard axis of Balogh-Joan Robinson-Galbraith has yielded pre-eminence to the Vienna-LSE-Virginia-Chicago alliance of Hayek-Robbins-Buchanan-Friedman. In universities, schools, journalism and (more slowly) broadcasting, the ablest, liveliest and younger, up-and-coming teachers, writers, commentators are predominantly in open intellectual rebellion against the post-war drift of collectivist economic theory and policy.

From a wide range of evidence, perhaps the most striking is the shift in direction of the once Tory-orthodox *Times* under the editorship of William Rees-Mogg who has become one of the most spirited and formidable exponents of liberal market philosophy. In a leading article, "On the side of liberty",[4] reviewing the "movement away from collectivism in the 1970s", it referred to the rise of the IEA "from *being regarded as* a marginal source of free economic propaganda to being a powerful centre of new ideas" (our italics) and acknowledged with engaging candour:

[4] *The Times,* 22 September, 1978.

"Again it is the old orthodoxy which is in decay; who can read Professor Galbraith without being astonished that we too once thought as he does now?"

What we are seeing, according to the leader writer, is nothing less than

". . . the strongest liberal reaction, asserting the rights of the individual against the state, that Britain has experienced since the early nineteenth century."

The percolation of these now commanding ideas can be seen most clearly in the new respect which even socialist-inclined politicians in all parties pay to the theory, if not always the practice, of monetary policy as a remedy for inflation. Allowing for differences in style and candour, Mr Callaghan has followed Sir Keith Joseph in rejecting the Keynesian hope that governments could pursue full employment by spending more money without causing inflation and intensifying unemployment. No less significant, prompted by the findings of public opinion polls, politicians of all parties have acknowledged that taxation is too high and that people are now more concerned with take-home pay than with the "social wage".

If it is still true that dominant ideas by Keynesian osmosis shape public policy, the evidence of the gradual but cumulative shift in opinion suggests it can be only a matter of time before the collectivist tide is decisively turned. As shown by this symposium, there are politicians in all three parties who would wish to respond to these changes by sharply re-directing policies towards freer choice in competitive markets. Yet, despite a general change of direction in the rhetoric of all parties, the official programme of none goes beyond arresting

the growth of government to dismantling the nationalised monopolies in hospitals, schools, universities, fuel,
transport, postal and other services that could serve the
public welfare better through what Hayek has called
"the discovery procedure of competition".

. . . OR DOMINANT INTERESTS?

Why do politicians in all three parties who understand
the case for a drastic pruning of central and local
government still shrink from acting more boldly on
their widely-shared beliefs? The answer they give (most
explicitly in private) is that, however economically
desirable such radical reform may be, it remains for the
present "politically impossible".

Some substance is given to this alibi for inaction by
the extension of market analysis to political and group
behaviour.[5] Thus during a century in which the "mixed
economy" has shifted ever further in conceding exemp-
tions from competition to sectional interests, politicians
have increasingly become the prisoners of lobbies whose
electoral support is judged necessary to secure the
decisive margin of votes required for victory. Thus the
interests entrenched by decades of creeping collectivism
have become the most formidable obstacle to its
eradication. It was this kind of analysis that led one of
our outstanding economic commentators, Mr Samuel
Brittan, to conclude a scholarly lecture at Chicago
University with this diagnosis[6] of the "English Sickness":

[5] *The Economics of Politics,* Readings 18, IEA, 1978.

[6] "How English is the English Sickness?", The eighth Henry
Simons Lecture, delivered at the University of Chicago Law
School, April 1978.

"The disease is that of collective action by special interest groups preventing a reasonably full use being made of our economic resources."

The paradox emerges that the pursuit of sectional enrichment by group interests is the major cause of Britain's impoverishment. More than any other factor, this analysis explains why average wages have fallen over fifty years from almost double German or French wages to little more than half. And the most self-defeating group interests—further entrenched by three decades of "full employment" at half efficiency—have undoubtedly been the restrictionist, backward-looking, "conservative" trade unions.[7]

A full reckoning of the damage union restrictionism has inflicted on the economy goes beyond their obstruction of innovation, efficiency, mobility and dependability of supply. Some indication of these costs is seen in the contrast between the decline of union-ridden dockland, Fleet Street, Clydeside, coalmines, motor cars, steel, and the expansion of services, typified by the internationally-acclaimed City of London, where enterprise is unimpeded by myopic trade unionism. Worse still, in recent years the increased legal, extra-legal and even illegal exertion of the unions' industrial, political and disruptive power has forced governments to pursue uneconomic and anti-economic policies of open and concealed subsidisation to bolster short-term phantom jobs at the expense of the long-term expansion in more efficient employment at higher real wages.

---

[7] *Trade Unions: Public Goods or Public 'Bads'?*, Readings 17, IEA, 1978.

DISARMAMENT OR CONFRONTATION?

Two hundred years ago Adam Smith drew encourage-
ment from the reflection that there is always "a deal of
ruin in a nation". In 1978 the ruin in the British
economy has spread so widely that all but the most
pampered sectional interests stand to gain from a
general economic disarmament. In place of the mounting civil war of all against all, we have to dismantle the
crude fortifications of producer protectionism. The
appropriate terms for a peace treaty would include
phasing-out legal and fiscal privileges from all but the
declining minority in need; replacing indiscriminate
welfare by a reverse income tax; strict control of the
money supply to stop inflation without the damaging
charade of prices and incomes policy; the massive with-
drawal of government to the frontier indicated by
public goods; a sharp reduction of central and local
governmental spending and a return of "public money"
to the private pockets whence it came; and the extension
of competitive markets to serve the consumer interest,
which is the only enduring economic interest the whole
community shares in common.

The chief obstacle to such a peaceful solution of the
battle between producer and consumer interests is the
entrenched monopoly power of trade unions. Yet objective analysis[8] shows that unions cannot raise the share
wages take from the national income above the market
value of labour's contribution to output except by
driving profits below their competitive level. In Britain
in 1978 it hardly needs elaboration that such an enforced
redistribution from capital to labour leads inexorably to

[8] W. H. Hutt, *The Theory of Collective Bargaining 1930-1975*,
Hobart Paperback 8, IEA, 1975.

reduced investment which in turn retards the growth in output, employment and other fruits of economic progress and prosperity—to the loss of workers no less than consumers. In addition, union monopoly causes further inefficiency through restrictions on entry and effort and through the dislocation of production by what Professor Hutt has called "the strike-threat system" or, more vividly, "the gun under the table".

In anything but the most narrow of short-term calculations, therefore, the highest interest of wage- and salary-earners is served by maximum competition between employers in a free labour market. Experience in non-unionised employments like those of secretaries, window-cleaners, pop stars, hairdressers, domestic helps—and cricketers since Packer—confirms that profit-powered competition offers better prospects of rising real incomes than the protective impedimenta of closed shops, bogus apprenticeships, over-manning, cutting-off essential supplies and other weapons of modern Luddism. The dilemma remains: how can the labour market work flexibly to spread the benefits of competitive efficiency so long as unions retain the legal privileges built up over a century and their leaders bask in political favours conferred by post-war governments? Having been armed to the teeth and anointed like medieval barons, will union leaders—or their more militant outriders—be restrained from open warfare, even by brotherly oaths of loyalty to the Labour Government, much less by an exchange of Christian names with those they regard as their political enemies?[9]

[9] A Conservative "shadow" Minister recently reported that union leaders had given assurances that they would work with him in government, adding: "I am on first-name terms with them". (*The Times*, 25 September, 1978.)

As the temporary truce of "incomes policy" gives way to pent-up market pressures, what is called "free collective bargaining" by union apologists (and unreflecting Conservatives) will increasingly be revealed as coercive, collectivist, confrontationist bargaining. The brute force of union power to raise wages above the market-clearing level might be partly checked by fear of bankrupting more employers and destroying still more jobs. But that residual discipline would be credible only so long as government resolutely refused to undo the mischief by subsidising jobs which unions had rendered uneconomic. And the unavoidable result would be rising long-term unemployment that must prove economically, socially and politically untenable. The choice is not the naïve one repeated by television journalists: to confront or not to confront? The decision is between confronting union monopoly now or drifting towards a still more imponderable and incalculable confrontation with multiplying victims of the power of union monopoly to complete its work of destruction in the motor industry, shipbuilding, mining, printing, steel, docks, hospitals, and even in what civil service unions ironically proclaim "public services".

THE ULTIMATE CHOICE

What are the alternatives? We cannot stand still even if we wished. It is a fallacy to suppose that the mixed economy is a stable equilibrium between market freedom and state servitude. The lesson of the relatively free economies we should emulate like West Germany, Japan, USA, Hong Kong is that even the most successful practitioners of limited government are under constant pressure to concede privileges to sectional interests that can only undermine the prosperity built up by economic freedom. As in Britain, there is a government multiplier at work whereby the failure of past interventions leads not to their removal but to their extension. Everywhere events have borne out Hayek's warning at the end of the war that, in the absence of a deliberate and sustained effort to move towards freedom, the mixed economy is remorselessly pushed further along "the road to serfdom". Sooner or later, a halt will have to be called and the later it is left the more disruptive it must be.

The real confrontation ahead for British people and their politicians is therefore with an inescapable choice between two sharply contrasting conceptions of the good society. The fully collectivist economy is based on a millenarian hope that imperfect human society can be democratically ruled by benign benevolence without the murderous malignancy that has overtaken all previous endeavours to establish a heaven on earth. Even without the testimony of history, economic analysis has shown the hope to be illusory. The alternative conception of an open free society[10] takes fallen man as he is and makes the best of an imperfect job by providing a structure of market incentives that harmonises as far as possible diverse individual purposes

[10]For those who share my belief in the primacy of spiritual values over economic "salvation", there need be no conflict with market economy. Unless we wish to impose our values on others (or risk others imposing their values on us), we should uphold the open society as alone permitting individuals to make their own choices and to accept responsibility for their own mortal and immortal destinies. These issues are brilliantly raised, though not resolved, by Arianna Stassinopoulos in *The Other Revolution*, Michael Joseph, London, 1978.

and leaves maximum scope for non-conformity, voluntary experimentation and personal fulfilment. Only the competitive economy and free society are compatible with the lawful operation of independent trade unions.

For all the amiable, human temptation to compromise and temporise, it is difficult to see how a confrontation with this choice can be much longer avoided. As Peter Jay argued shortly before taking refuge in the British Embassy in Washington,[11] the tensions in our collectivist-corporatist political economy are far more severe and endemic than is widely understood or publicly acknowledged. The tug-of-war between insatiable sectional interests and the economic reality of scarce resources has been prevented from pulling society apart only by astute alternations between the unsustainable illusions of inflation, foreign borrowing, North Sea oil and repeatedly deferred promises. The providential state must always disappoint the demands upon it because they are based *au fond* on a rebellion against the limitations of the human condition itself.

Avoidably high unemployment, rising prices and excessive government spending are all the time weakening the market sector and carrying the economy closer to a degree of collectivism for which the electorate never voted and which it shows no signs of wanting. Political democracy is mocked by unlimited government which inevitably produces an outcome that satisfies none yet offers no certain means of peaceful reversal. Hence the case for entrenched limitations on the power of party politicians to concede short-term electoral

[11]*Employment, Inflation and Politics,* Occasional Paper 46, IEA, 1976.

favours that raise long-term spectres of an unmanage-
able economy and ungovernable polity. Such a constitutional revolution to tame over-mighty political
subjects would almost certainly require time for a
radical re-alignment of the party system. Meanwhile,
the more immediate issue is whether the open society
can be prevented from further closing to the point
where if two parties remain it will be on Lenin's terms
of one party in power and the other in prison. That is
the stark but ultimate reality of the choice the British
people must now prepare to confront.

INDEX